| DATE DUE | | |
|---|---|---|
| FEB 0 3 1998 SEP 0 3 1996 | 3-25-04 | |
| MAR 1 8 1999 | | |
| OCT 1 8 1999 | | |
| FEB 0 5 2000 FEB 1 5 2000 | | |
| MAR 1 3 2000 | | |
| JUL 2 3 2001 | | |

IDENTIFICATION REQUIRED                    COPY20

792.022   Holtje, Adrienne.
H          Putting on the school play : a com-
       plete handbook / Adrienne Kriebel
       Holtje and Grace A. Mayr. -- West
       Nyack, N.Y. : Parker Pub. Co., c1980.
       216p. ill.
          ISBN 0-13-744649-7  14.95

       1.College and school drama. 2.Amateur
       theatricals--Production and direction.
       3.Children's plays--Presentation, etc.
       1.Mayr, Grace A., 1910-       jt. auth.

# Putting On The
# School Play:
# A COMPLETE HANDBOOK

# Putting On The School Play:

## A COMPLETE HANDBOOK

Adrienne Kriebel Holtje

AND

Grace A. Mayr

PARKER PUBLISHING COMPANY, INC. • WEST NYACK, N.Y.

© 1980 *by*

Parker Publishing Company, Inc.
West Nyack, New York

**Library of Congress Cataloging in Publication Data**

Holtje, Adrienne.
   Putting on the school play.

   Includes index.
   1.  College and school drama.  2.  Amateur
theatricals--Production and direction.  3.  Children's
plays--Presentation, etc.  I.  Mayr, Grace A.,
1910-    joint author.  II.  Title.
PN3178.P7H6      792'.0226        79-21165
ISBN 0-13-744649-7

**Printed in the United States of America**

# ACKNOWLEDGMENTS

Strand Century . . .A company within the Rank Organization, for their lighting information and their kind permission to use photos of their equipment.

H. Walter Struck . . .Art Instructor, Riverdell Middle School, Oradell, New Jersey, for his directions on how to make papier-mâché masks and objects.

*Plays,* the *Drama Magazine for Young People.* . . for kind permission to reprint a portion of the play, *One Man in His Time,* by Grace A. Mayr.

# How This Book Will Help You Put On A Winning School Play...Every Time

Do you, like so many other teachers, find that putting on a school play is a grueling experience? Even if drama was your major, you may face problems that seem insurmountable because of technical details, lack of student interest, and the chain of mini-crises that seem to plague every school play. If it's any consolation, you're not alone.

To help you, we have written this book. It's the product of a lot of experience with school plays. It's chock-full of teacher-tested techniques, helpful hints and ingenious solutions to the problems that seem to occur when you least expect them. Because you are one of the busiest people in the world—we know a teacher's load—this book has been organized in step-by-step fashion to take you through the school play from the pre-production meeting to the last curtain call, and even the clean-up after the audience has left.

Whether you're an experienced drama coach, or you are faced with your first play, this book will provide fresh ideas on coaching methods, costume and stage design, lighting and special effects and dozens of practical, easy-to-use shortcuts that will help you make stars of your students and enhance your professional reputation.

### HERE ARE SOME SPECIFIC WAYS THIS BOOK
### WILL HELP MAKE YOUR PLAYS SUCCESSFUL...

* The right play—and you. If there ever was a winning combination, this is it. But how do you know when you have the

right play? If you use the unique five-step outline we give you in Chapter 1, your chances of success will be multiplied.

* What do you do if your students want to create their own play? Ordinarily this situation is filled with problems—unless you use our Magic Seven Guidelines to Creative Dramatics.

* Not everyone can be the star. And there are times when those who don't make it can make trouble. Do you know how to handle this; how to turn a potential disaster into the season's dramatic success? We do, and we will show you how others have done it successfully.

* Did you know that there is one simple way that is more effective than anything else you may do to keep the production on schedule? It's all detailed on our success-tested 20-day production calendar.

* You may have the best actors in the school, but your play could flop because of the failure of your backstage crew. Learn how to make sure that these people, as well as your front-of-house staff, work as hard as your actors.

* How many rehearsals? There is a system that works, and we will tell you how many you should have, what should be accomplished at each, and how to evaluate the performance of the actors as well as every member of the supporting staff.

* Do you face some tricky script problems? Profanity? Smoking? Drinking, and even love scenes? They can all be handled to everyone's satisfaction without sacrificing the play, if you follow our suggestions.

* Somewhere, about halfway from the first meeting to opening night, it seems that everyone—including you—will have "had it." No matter what you think or do, all you and many of the others want is out. What do you do to overcome this common problem? We have the answer.

* We even have some ideas to help you improve your actors' diction and projection.

* What if you don't have a stage? Read Chapter 5 on Staging the Play . . . Your Showcase For Talent, and find out how to make one yourself.

* Perhaps the biggest problem most teachers face is that of costuming the play. We have solved this for you once and for all with a unique multi-purpose costume pattern that can be used to clothe any character in any historical period.

* As far as stage props are concerned, you can literally make a silk purse out of a sow's ear when you read Chapter 9. We will tell you how to make anything that you cannot beg, borrow or rent.

* What do you do if the script calls for an offstage explosion? It's simple, and we show you how to make everything from the eruption of Krakatoa to a pistol shot, lightning and rolling thunder.

* School plays can cost money. If you refer to the fiscal problem-solver we have presented in Chapter 12, the chances are that you will come in on or under budget every time. Such success doesn't go unnoticed in terms of your professional reputation.

In addition to all this, you will find many examples, checklists, professional tips and references that will make your job not only easy, but will make it so much fun that you may want to do another play before the semester is over.

Happy theatre.

A.K.H.
G.A.M

# CONTENTS

# Putting On The
# School Play:
## A COMPLETE HANDBOOK

# CHAPTER 1

# Successful Ways to Select
# Your School Play

The right play and you—that's the winning combination. How do you find this right play? Easy.

First of all, realize that the perfectly right play doesn't exist. Settle for a play that you can make right by good directing, and most of all, for a play that you like and will enjoy directing.

The importance of choosing this right play is rather like the importance of choosing the right traveling companion for a long journey. Since you'll be living with this play for a long period of time (four weeks according to this book's plan), you and the play must be compatible.

Long before this four-week period (with its tight schedule for casting, for making up your director's book, for the 15 rehearsals and the performance), even months ahead, choose the play.

Just as you would need to know your destination before setting out on a journey, so you need to know the kind of play you're looking for in order to find it.

## FIVE SURE-FIRE STEPS FOR A CLEAR, STRAIGHTFORWARD ROUTE TO SUCCESS IN CHOOSING YOUR PLAY

### First Step

Consider these six determining factors which affect your choice of play:

1. *The Occasion*—Is the play to be:

— a middle-school assembly program for pupils only,

— a money-raiser for the scholarship fund with a paying audience,

— a demonstration of primary pupils' work for a parent-teacher meeting,

— the traditional senior class play staged as part of a class night celebration,

— a round-the-table reading play of a literary classic, written and presented in your school auditorium by an English class at the afternoon session of the County Language Arts Association, or

— your school system's contribution to a civic festival on the commons, commemorating an anniversary of the founding of the town?

The right play suits the occasion.

2. *The Audience*—Since without an audience there can be no play, the play must be chosen with the prospective audience in mind. Notice how the type of audience varies in each occasion mentioned previously.

Those lively middle-schoolers want entertainment, more action than talk (a requirement wisely applied to any school play), and they want laughs.

The paying audience of pupils, teachers, friends and relations and public sponsors of the scholarship fund also wants to be pleased, and expects and deserves a competent performance for its money. The fond parents and relatives who provide the audience at a lower school PTA meeting indulgently accept a less polished piece of creative dramatics made up by the children from their own experience or from a favorite story.

The class night audience, celebrating and highly uncritical of the play committee's presentation, is an anything-goes crowd, ready to laugh at a split infinitive.

On the other hand, the professional assemblage of language arts teachers is a very different audience, hypercritical not only of the literary quality of the play, but also of the pedagogical value of creative dramatics as a teaching method.

The heterogeneous crowd your actors play to at the anniversary festivals, possibly from a temporary open-air stage in the football stadium or a public park, is a mobile, good-natured throng easily distracted from the performance by a plane passing overhead, the late arrival of a public figure with a motor escort, the balloon vendor—anything and everything.

Keep in mind that a play is played before an audience and must please that audience. Know your potential audience in order to choose the right play for that audience.

3. *Playing Time*—As occasion and audience differ, so the playing time allowed for the performance varies. A long, full-length play, suitable for grades 8-12, runs 1½ hours to 1¾ hours, including changing of scenery, with the two-act play growing in popularity. The "two-acter" achieves greater unity and continuity of action than the familiar three-act play, since the intermission is merely a brief midway break for the audience to relax and chat with friends until the play resumes. A one-act play runs 15 to 45 minutes, ideally between 20 and 25 minutes. Figure a page of dialog at a minute and a half. Fifteen pages make up into a neat "one-acter." The occasion for the play often limits the playing time.

The middle school assembly play, the class night play, the civic festival play—all should play no longer than 25 minutes, the ideal maximum for a one-acter.

The demonstration at the PTA meeting may play as briefly as 10 minutes or extend to 18 to 20 minutes, depending upon the age of the performers—the younger, the shorter.

The scholarship fund money-raiser, if it is the sole attraction of the program, could play 90 minutes or so.

The round-the-table reading play, a more static performance—the readers tell, don't perform the action of the play—in a 20-to-35-minute reading period can condense the action of a long classic novel or drama, or offer an original full-life story of a famous person.

You'll need to know the playing time limitations you must meet before you can choose the play.

The playing time of too long or too short a script can always be altered by telescoping lines and deleting minor characters, or by writing in more characters and dialog. Remember always: *Rather too short than too long. Leave your audience laughing and wanting more.*

4. *Actors*—Playwrights often write plays with certain actors in mind. William Shakespeare is believed to have created roles to

fit the particular acting genius of each man and boy among the King's Men, his players.

Before you choose your play, you must have in mind the sex, age, and number of players available to you. Will you be working with an all-girl cast, an all-boy cast, a mixed cast, six to eight-year-olds, middle-schoolers aged nine to 12, young adults? Good plays for any of these categories are available.

With young children you'll find no lack of actors. Boys and girls alike are eager to put on a play. Among juniors (9-12) and young adults (12 and up), you'll find more eager actresses than actors. Knowing this, today's playwrights of school plays are writing plays that have more female than male roles.

You can solve the problem of too many male roles in any play you choose. Characters can always have a sex change with a bit of rewriting. Turn a male character into a female character and update the script with a female letter-carrier, taxi driver, plumber, etc. Women are into everything these days and would be pleased to see these roles played by females, especially young ones.

Choose a play not over-weighted with aged characters, which young performers find difficult to play well.

Should you find that you have more willing and able actors than roles in the play you'd like to direct, simply add walk-ons, remembering to write these minor parts into the script and to assign each one simple lines and stage business in keeping with the mood and the story line of the play. If you have fewer actors than roles, have some of the cast play more than one part. This is called *doubling,* a theatre ploy as old as drama itself.

In the case of all girls to direct, choose an all-girl play or assign girls to play males roles—something that rarely works well, however. Rather, borrow males from another class or club to play the male roles.

In the case of all boys to direct, choose an all-boy play or cast boys in the female roles—something that has always worked. Boy actors played all of the female roles on the Elizabethan stage. In fact, at that time an all-boy children's company successfully rivaled the men's companies in popularity. The first professional actresses didn't appear on the English stage until the 17th century.

5. *Acting Area* (stage) *and Its Equipment*—Where the play is to be performed and what technical equipment this area offers are

important factors in choosing the right play. Will your actors be performing:

- On a picture-frame stage with a curtain, a lighting board, etc., in the school auditorium (the ideal situation),
- On the gymnasium floor on a temporary stage with no curtain, only makeshift spotlights rigged up on portable stanchions and with the audience sitting on three sides; in effect, an open stage,
- In a public hall with a platform perhaps, but with meager lighting equipment and no curtain,
- On the hillside lawn behind the public library,
- On the steps of a municipal building, or
- On an improvised stage with a narrator speaking over a public address system on the town commons or in the football stadium?

In view of all these varied possibilities, choose a play that requires only one simple set (for example: indoors, living room, den or attic; outdoors; porch, park, garden, town hall steps or whatever the locale of the stage area demands) with a minimum of lighting effects and no sound effects, if possible.

## TYPES OF PLAYS: TRAGEDY, COMEDY, FARCE, PUPPET, SHADOW, PANTOMIME, ROUND-THE-TABLE READING, CREATIVE DRAMATICS

Take your choice. The range is wide.

*Tragedy*—Serious drama where the protagonist is defeated by the opposing forces. This is probably the easiest for amateurs to perform, but the least fun for either actors or audience.

*Comedy*—Light drama where the happy ending is guaranteed. This is undoubtedly the next to easiest for amateurs to perform and the most likely to succeed. Comedy outplays serious drama by four to one.

*Farce* (melodrama)—Despite the fun this type provides both actors and audience, it is probably the hardest for amateurs to perform well because almost perfect timing is required to sustain the slapstick humor based on exaggerated and farfetched situations and characters.

*Puppet Show*—Puppetry is a special branch of the drama. If you've had personal experience with puppet shows and are a skilled puppeteer yourself, go blithely ahead. Nothing is more fun for all—the puppeteers and the audience—than a well-produced puppet show, one of the oldest forms of drama. Hand puppets, rather than stick or string marionettes, are more popular with young performers because they're familar toys and fairly easy to operate. A puppet show is as effective outdoors as indoors, but requires the audience to be in close proximity to the puppet stage.

*Shadow Play*—This ancient type of drama, that reached its peak of perfection in 1000 B.C. in China, requires special skills of operators. These shadow puppeteers squat before a lamp behind a screen, manipulating over their heads figures controlled by wooden sticks attached to the arms and legs of the puppets. The audience sees only the moving shadows on the screen. All in all, it is not the type of play to choose unless you have personally worked with shadow puppets or have time to learn the necessary skills before embarking upon a school production.

*Pantomime*—No words are spoken in this type of drama. Actors convey their meaning by silent gestures, exaggerated to a larger-than-life scale. Heads bob deeply, bodies shudder with convulsive sighs, arms waved grandiosely. Pantomime is a form much less popular with audiences than plays with dialogue. Most people, children in particular, like a play "with talking" better. Pure pantomime is best left to the professionals. A combination of pantomime and oral narration, however, is a good possibility.

The anniversary festival play, perhaps created for the occasion by a talented local writer, would work out well with a narrator using a microphone to relate the story of the founding of the town and its growth throughout the years while appropriately costumed performers played it out on a stage in the center of the football stadium. Since noises are permissible in pantomime as sound effects, enlivening features of this drama might be whooping native war cries, a barrage of rifle shots, the ringing of church bells, or cheers for historic heroes in the script. Absolute necessities for a production of this sort would be a first-class public address system and a skillful narrator, who is an excellent oral reader and is able to achieve a vital spontaneity in delivery of the prepared script, so that the words don't sound machine-uttered.

*Round-the-Table Reading Play*—A professionally written round-the-table reading play is without doubt the easiest drama type to produce. A narrator, again an unhurried, good oral reader, is needed, one who gives the audience time to think and react to the full force of the words as he relates the transitional action that carries the play smoothly from scene to scene. Copies of the script lie before the actor-readers, who sit around a table (three sides only, so their faces are visible and their voices audible at all times.) Very few rehearsals are needed, certainly not 15 (see Chapter 4)—perhaps three rehearsals will do. No memorizing of lines, no blocking of action, no costuming and no special effects are needed. The literary and educational value of this type of drama is high, but its money-making potential is low.

*Creative Dramatics*—This do-it-yourself type of drama is best used for production with young children five to eight, and best played in a classroom, a library, or a not-too-large meeting room. With any class of this most uninhibited, naturally creative age group of school children, you can put together a quite charming informal 10 to 15-minute playlet dramatizing a favorite story that an audience of their peers or their parents and relatives will love. The writing of the script should predate the performance by a goodly period of time. Several weeks or months are needed, for this process is always time-consuming and hard on the teacher, who not only "writes," but also directs; thereby doubling the work of putting on a school play.

## SEVEN MAGIC GUIDELINES TOWARD CREATIVE DRAMATICS

There are times, however, when no other type play will do; so here are the Magic Seven guidelines for you and your young co-authors:

1. Start with a good story—an original one made up by the children, or a legend, a myth, a folk or fairy tale, a historical adventure, an animal story, etc.

2. Be sure everyone likes the story and thinks it will be fun to dramatize.

3. Know the story well.

4.  Act it out several times, with whoever wants to play the parts, to make up the lines and the action.

5.  As the one best qualified, write down the lines and the action everyone decides are the best, carefully editing the material into a playable 10 to 50-minute script.

6.  Prepare three more copies of the finished script than there are speaking parts: one for each player (if the child can't read, for the player's parent to help the child learn lines); one for your own use as director; one for your files; and one for the prompter.

7.  Wait to cast the play until the performance is scheduled.

Creating plays from their favorite stories or from their own experiences is of immeasurable value to young children, for it awakens in them an appreciation of what making up and acting in a play is all about. But a school play where admission is charged and the public is invited must meet higher and stricter dramatic standards, and offer more audience entertainment than such informal creative drama affords. Quality entertainment—the essence of good theatre—is more readily found in published plays written by professionals. As a professional in education, you understand this and respect professionalism in every field. Creative dramatics has its limitations.

### Second Step (on the route to the right play)

Come to a decision on the requirements of your right play, and on a 4" x 6" index card organize and fill out a checklist with specific data about that right play. For example:

### THE RIGHT PLAY

*Occasion*

The headline one-act attraction of a school-sponsored program held to raise money to buy new uniforms for the ball teams.

*Audience*

A paying audience of pupils, teachers, friends and the general public.

*Playing Time*

20 to 35 minutes; the evening's program (8:00 to 10:00 P.M.) is to include musical numbers by the school band, a pep rally led

by the cheerleaders, and a presentation of the ball teams and their coaches.

*Actors*

Seven to 10 (male and female) speaking parts.

*Stage and Equipment*

Curtained stage, with lighting board for overheads and spotlights, in school auditorium. The seating capacity on main floor and in gallery is 500.

*Type of Play*

Contemporary comedy with one simple set, a young cast with an equal number of male and female roles, a minimum of lighting effects, and no sound or special effects, if possible.

**Third Step**

Issue a call for a meeting:

1. through the front office daily bulletin,
2. over the intercom,
3. in a notice posted in the students' lounge, or
4. by whatever means of general announcement you like, to all pupils interested in serving on the play committee to help choose the forthcoming play for the benefit performance. Include the time and place; for example, *Thursday, directly after school, in Room 256.*

Skip this step and also steps 4 and 5 with younger children (5-8), where it's best if the play choice is not prompted by their classwork or the season of the year, that you autocratically choose the play yourself. With young players their instant delight in the suggestion *"Let's put on a play"* is always enough to arouse their immediate enthusiasm for the play of your choice.

With juniors (9-12) and seniors (12 and up) this step is optional, but recommended as a more democratic means of selecting the play. The play committee, however, is merely to help by suggesting plays, since young people who are still in the process of developing their standards of artistic, literary, and dramatic taste have often not gained sufficient knowledge through experience to discriminate between the worthwhile and the specious. Although you would never wish to assume the role of a dictator, you must assume the responsibility for making the final decision.

### Fourth Step

Meet with the play committee as announced. Keep the meeting brief, but cover these three points:

1. Distribute copies of your checklist of specific data about the right play.
2. Discuss the six items on the checklist.
3. Suggest these sources of the play (where you plan to look also):

— School reading textbooks.
— Collections of plays and singly bound plays in the school and public libraries.
— *Plays, The Drama Magazine for Young People,* 8 Arlington Street, Boston, Massachusetts 02116. Copies are usually available on the racks of the school library and of the children's room in the public library. On the inside of the back cover of each of the year's eight issues are listed titles from past issues for special days in that month, separated into subject and school-age categories. (Catalog is available free on request.) For subscribers, the plays may be produced royalty-free and no written permission is necessary. For nonsubscribers and professional companies charging admission, application must be made in writing for royalty quotations and permission to produce any of the plays.
— Catalogs of play publishers, usually available in the public library. If not, the reference librarian can supply the addresses of play publishers to whom you can write for their current catalogs.

### Fifth Step

Meet again with the play committee. Pool suggestions of the members with those of your own. You may have as many as five titles. If one is a musical, eliminate it at once. Musical plays with singing and dancing should be produced by the school's Music and Physical Education Departments, whose heads, not you, make the choice of play. Narrow the remainder down by measuring each play against the checklist until only one play is left. If you like this play well enough to direct it, that play is the right play. Remembering your director's responsibility to make the final decision, make your choice with a high heart. You have the right play.

## A DIRECTOR'S GUIDE TO SCHOOL
## PLAY PUBLISHERS

Directors of school theatrical productions are constantly on the lookout for new and exciting plays. Over the years, we have found several play publishers to whom the teacher-director may go to find suitable plays for all levels.

Let us share them with you:

Art Craft Play Company, Box 1830, Cedar Rapids, Iowa 52406

> One- and three-act plays for junior and senior high. Royalties are required for the privilege of staging any play. Catalog and annual mailing to all junior and senior high schools are available free on request.

Baker's Plays, 100 Chauncy Street, Boston, Massachusetts 02111

> One-, two- and three-act children's plays, theatre anthologies, and entertainments. Royalty due on royalty-charged plays when staged before an audience. No royalty is charged on one-act plays presented within the school to students and faculty only, with no invited guests. A reduction in royalty fee is offered on full-length plays presented within the school to students and faculty only, with no invited guests. Catalog is available free on request.

Eldridge Publishing Company, Franklin, Ohio 45005

> One- and three-act plays for schools. When royalty plays are given, the royalty is due regardless of whether or not admission is charged— an arrangement based on Eldridge Publishing Company's relationship with its authors. Catalog is available free on request.

Samuel French, Inc., 25 West 45th Street, New York, New York 10036

> One-, two-, three-act plays for all ages—children to senior citizens. Royalty fees vary. Terms for all performances are quoted on application. In the catalog see the material on "Budget Plays" produced by amateurs *for one stage performance only*. Catalog is available free on request.

Heuer Publishing Company, Box 248, Cedar Rapids, Iowa 52406

> One- and three-act plays for junior and senior high. Royalties are required for the privilege of staging any play. Catalog and annual mailing to all junior and senior high schools are available free on request.

Plays, Inc. Publishers, 8 Arlington Street, Boston, Massachusetts 02116

> Book collections and singly bound copies of royalty-free one-act

plays for the lower and middle grades, junior and senior high. Catalogs are available free on request.

Performance Publishing Company, 978 North McLean Boulevard, Elgin, Illinois 60120

One-, two-, and three-act plays for grade schools and junior and senior high schools. Royalty fees are listed in the catalog and on page two of each play book published. Royalty rate is automatically reduced when no admission to the performance is charged. Catalog is available free on request.

*Note:*   Royalty Fees and Permission to Produce

The legal requirements of paying royalty fees (payment of a fixed sum for each performance) and of asking permission to produce a play are the director's responsibility.

On the title page of a singly bound play and on the back of the title page in a collection of plays, appear the copyright date and an "All Rights Reserved" caution against the illegal use of the plays. You may also find a "Notice for Amateur Production" reading like this:

> "These plays may be produced by schools, clubs and similar
> amateur groups without payment of a royalty fee."

If so, this is good news for you. No royalty fee to increase production costs!

Also on this same page may appear a "Notice for Professional Production," which means any form of non-amateur presentation (professional stage, radio, television), advising that permission to produce any of the plays must be obtained in writing from the publisher, whose address is given. Permission may or may not involve a royalty fee, but permission must be obtained.

Study all references to royalty and permission to produce in the play publishers' catalogs to avoid later embarrassment and disappointment. In every catalog you'll find a notice regarding royalties, which states clearly the right procedure concerning payment of royalty fees, writing for and securing permission to produce before scheduling a production, and acknowledging authorship credit on programs and on all advertising for the scheduled play.

With some play publishing companies, amateurs seeking permission to present a play *for one stage performance only* may be excused from payment of a royalty fee provided the producer purchases as many copies of the play as there are speaking parts in the script.

Check with the utmost care the royalty information in each catalog. Failure to honor this indebtedness to the publisher and to the playwright, whose time and talent created the play you want to produce, and failure to write for permission to produce the play are illegal.

**Let's Review:**

1.  Start early, long before the production is scheduled.

2.  Use a specification sheet for the play you're seeking, listing these determining factors: occasion, audience, playing time, actors, stage and equipment, and type of play.

3.  If directing young children (5-8), choose the play yourself. If directing juniors (9-12) or seniors (12 and up), work with a play committee, but, as the director's right, reserve for yourself the privilege (and responsibility) of making the final choice.

4.  Know your legal obligations in the matter of paying royalty fees and of obtaining in writing the acting rights for the play chosen.

Once you've chosen your play and understand your obligations (if any) to a play publisher, immediately tackle the three routine matters discussed in the beginning of our next chapter.

# CHAPTER 2

# Seventeen Helpful Ideas on Casting Your Play

### Pinpointing the Time to Start Casting

As soon as the calendar reveals that the scheduled production date is four weeks—20 school days—off, cast the play, allowing two of these 20 days for the tryouts.

### Three Matters to Tackle Before Casting

First, however, take care of three routine tasks:

1. *As soon as the play is chosen,* see to acquiring the needed playscripts. If you're working with a do-it-yourself or a student-written script, requisition through the supply department that copies be duplicated on the office machines either in the business department or clerical office of your school. You'll need a copy for each member of the cast, one for the prompter and two for you. (Remember, one copy is for your files.) If you purchase playbooks from a play publishing company, order one for each member of the cast, two for the prompter's book, and two for your director's book. (Details for making up both books are supplied in Chapter 3.) Remember also to get in writing permission to produce the play, and to pay any required first royalty fee.

2. *As soon as you have a copy of the script,* start working on your director's book (See Chapter 3), even though much of this book depends upon the casting results. At this point, you're particularly interested in cast requirements, characterizations and in making any character alterations such as sex, age, nationality or race.

*3. As soon as you have made a fair start on your director's book,* sign up any production personnel (friendly, helpful colleagues) that you can recruit; for example, the art teacher, the sewing teacher, the shop teacher, the print teacher, a classroom teacher or a school subject teacher—the more the merrier.

## Director's Choice

Now to cast your play!

If you're to direct actors aged five to eight, choose the players yourself, being guided by the interest of the children and their enthusiasm for certain parts. You know best their abilities and limitations, their personalities and their growth needs. They feel secure with you and will accept the assignment of parts that you make.

## Simplified Casting

Casting the round-the-table reading play resolves itself very simply. You need good oral readers. Cast your best for the major roles, fill the other parts with volunteers, even less able readers, and let the three rehearsals you'll direct for the public reading be lessons in phrasing, enunciation, interpretation and projection—in effect, possibly the finest teaching of your career.

## You 9-Point Guide to the Open Tryout

If you're preparing to cast juniors (9-12) or seniors (12 and up), here's a clear-cut, nine-point positive approach that gives the greatest opportunity to the greatest number, and the widest choice possible for you—the open tryout, where anyone reads for the part he or she wants.

## Clear-Cut Methods of Working with a Casting Committee

1. Organize a casting committee, as diversified a group as possible, of some of those teacher-friends already signed up to help, and of some interested pupils, perhaps one or two of the play committee who won't be trying out for parts. In casting, as in all production matters, you retain maximum responsibility and have the final word in the selection of the players for every role, although you make good use of reliable and valid help.

2. Call a casting committee meeting to arrange such mechanics of the tryouts as:

*Place*—a classroom or the stage of the school auditorium or any area with cleared floor space and a way to exclude casual spectators who may embarrass the candidates.

*Time*—two days to guarantee a fair audition for all candidates.

*Briefing or casting committee*—discussion of the characters in the play, the major and minor roles, to familiarize the committee with the casting needs:

    a. The number of male and female roles.

    b. The importance of casting major roles first. Minor, perhaps better called supporting, roles are more easily cast and may be filled by the runners-up for major roles.

    c. The physical characteristics to be considered, such as height, weight, looks, personality, mannerisms. The male lead, Roger Strongheart, ought not to be smaller or less robust than his arch enemy Murgatroyd Dangerfield. Merrylips Lovely ought not to be cast to play the bony-fingered, warty-faced bad fairy in *Sleeping Beauty*. There is a limit to what costume and make-up can do.

    d. Understudies. Understudies rarely get a chance to perform except in old Hollywood movies, but being prepared with one or two actors who can step in at the last minute to play an important role is invaluable insurance against castastrophe.

In short, once the details are arranged for the tryouts you can move ahead quickly.

3. Announce the time and place of the tryouts and where copies of the play are available on the main hall bulletin board, in the daily notice from the front office, over the intercom, at an assembly program and/or in the school newspaper.

4. Put copies of the script in the school library, where candidates can read the play, select the roles that interest them, and study the lines before auditioning. Collect these copies in time for the tryouts.

5. At the tryouts, register the names of the candidates upon arrival and ask what parts they prefer. Welcome each candidate, cautioning all that anyone chosen for a part must agree to give up any other extra activity for the next four weeks, for the play's the thing! If all have not read the play, outline the plot, describe the setting and give enough information about the characters so that the candidates can appreciate the parts to be read.

6. Instruct the candidates to wait in another place, pre-

viously designated, within easy call, and then with the casting committee audition each candidate, who is permitted to read a passage
either he or she has chosen or one you choose.  The order in which
candidates are called may be alphabetical (You have their names
on slips or cards.) or by random pulling of their names from a
container by a member of the casting committee.  Thank each
candidate after the audition, but make no decisions until all tryouts
are over.  You don't want to be fooled by the virtuoso reading of a
part by a flash-in-the-pan kind of candidate, as he or she may be
superficially adept and not have the sensitivity to respond deeply to
the nuances of the role.  Give close attention to that confused,
awkward, diffident boy or girl, all burning aspirations and therefore
so teachable and so coach-able—attend the one who reads indiffer-
ently this first time, but may possess a potential skill for the part
he or she wants that you will discover or uncover by sympathetic
direction. All any actor needs, besides some talent, of course, are
intelligence and a will to learn.

The tryouts may take two days.  There may be some candidates you'll want to hear a second time.

7.  When all the candidates have had their chance to
read parts, dismiss them, and discuss the casting with the casting
committee.

Certain questions help in casting a role:

a. Who fills the part best?

b. Does he or she have that special quality (call it charisma,
   personal magnetism, an unexplainable mystery of certain
   personalities) that springs across the footlights to enchant
   the audience?

c. Does he or she look the part?

d. Does he or she have a good record of reliability and punctu-
   ality, of yielding center stage to others, and of enjoying
   teamwork?

e. Would he or she, if cast in a minor role, make a good under-
   study for a major role?  Such casting, if possible, is helpful
   in the event of an emergency.  Skiing accidents do happen;
   legs do break!  Minor roles are usually easily filled.

With the help of the casting committee, cast the major roles
first, then the minor roles and understudies (Runners-up make

excellent understudies), drawing up a tentative cast for your further consideration and final decision.

8. On the day after tryouts close, make your final decision on the best possible cast from all the candidates. Also, now is the time to do a bit of checking and to improve public relations:

   a. Check with the teachers of the actors you have chosen for the parts to make sure these pupils may profitably devote the next four weeks to play-acting without serious loss to their studies. You'll find that the good will thus enlisted from these teachers is comforting to have.

   b. Telephone the parents of the same pupils to make sure the parents are willing to allow their children to give the rehearsal time required. You should use this fine opportunity to engage the help of willing parents at some of those production jobs where they're beyond price—making costumes, supervising make-up, etc. (particularly if the parent has had some previous stage experience, even amateur). In your director's book keep a list of the names and addresses of these willing parents for easy reference.

9. All that remains now is to list the cast with understudies and publish it by posting it on the main hall bulletin board with a call for the first rehearsal, specifying time and place.

### Ensuring Acceptance of the Director's Final Decision

Adhere faithfully to this method of the open tryout, where all comers receive equal opportunity, and winners and losers alike will accept the results with good grace and no hurt feelings.

Should any minor actor's ego need bolstering later during rehearsal, you can always quote Stanislavsky of the Moscow Art Theatre (the Method genius): "There are no small parts, only small actors."

### A Director's Blueprint for Including the Losers in the Production

To ease some of the natural disappointment those who fail to get parts must feel, publish alongside the cast listing and the first rehearsal call, an offer to them of first consideration for jobs on the production staff, the following being a sampling of the various jobs open: stage manager, stage hand, lighting director, publicity head, business manager.

As the work progresses into the next phase, they'll all soon realize that there is no time for stars—that putting on a play, like all creative experience, is by nature cooperative teamwork, that the whole production is more important than any one of its separate parts.

**Let's Review:**

Two good rules of thumb for successful casting are:

1. Cast the play yourself with young players (5-8) and use the open tryout with older players (9 and up).
2. Welcome advice, but make all final casting decisions yourself.

The best script in the world and the most talented cast are nothing in themselves without a drama coach to mastermind the play's production. All aspects of your versatile job as teacher-director are clearly and simply spelled out for you in our next chapter.

# CHAPTER 3

# How to Master Your Role As Director of the Production

"Directing a play is more than just getting the actors to speak their parts," a high school student director admitted on opening night of his first play—a free, out-of-doors, student-run production of Shakespeare's *A Midsummer Night's Dream*.

True! Directing a play is like composing a symphony, writing a novel, designing a house, or more basically, like making a birthday cake. The director gathers the ingredients (script, cast, backstage crew, business staff, volunteer helpers); combines them in the right order and proportion (with rehearsals and staff meetings; costumes, properties, lights; telephone calls and individual conferences); and adds flavoring (instruction, encouragement, praise, whatever best seasons the play). Then the director bakes the mixture for the given time (See rehearsal schedule); tops it with artistry (the director's own uniquely personal interpretation of the tone, mood and theme of the play); and serves the confection (a finished performance) to the birthday guests (the audience).

As director of a school play you are not only its drama coach "getting the actors to speak their parts," but also its mastermind with fingertip control of all phases of the production; executive enough to delegate duties, but smart enough to check and recheck progress systematically so that "things get done."

Well then, you've got things done so far, haven't you? You've chosen the play. You've cast it. You've lined up workers for the production staff. Now, you have more plan-ahead plotting to do to work out the play as fully as possible before rehearsals start.

Start by drawing up the rehearsal schedule, a 20 school-day calendar. Three of these 20 days you've already used up in casting, recruiting staff and beginning your director's book.

A tight, nicely trimmed, but adequate 20-day calendar looks like this (Figure 3-1).

To get your show on the road faster and to help you produce a finished performance with a professional look, spend the fourth day of your 20-day rehearsal schedule working mainly on your director's book.

## "LUCKY SEVEN"—THE DIRECTIONS
## FOR MAKING UP YOUR DIRECTOR'S BOOK

Follow these lucky seven simple directions and you'll have a workable blueprint for every detail of the production:

1. Use a three-ringed, loose-leaf, hard-cover binder (overall size 9½" x 11½").

If you're working with a typescript, punch three notebook holes in each page, apply a reinforcement ring to each hole, and lock the script between the covers of the binder. You have ample room in the margins and on the back of each page for your notes and sketches.

If more space is needed, add blank pages (8½" x 11").

If you're working with a printed script (professionally published playbook), you'll need two copies. Use the same binder and 8½" x 11" mounting paper. Cut apart both copies of the play-book. Paste or tape page one from the first playbook to a sheet of mounting paper; paste or tape page two from the second playbook on the second mounting sheet. Page one of the first playbook is now face down on a mounting sheet. You see why you need two copies.) Continue until all pages of the play are mounted. Punch the needed holes in each sheet, and lock these mounted pages in their proper sequence into the binder. Since playbooks are usually 5" x 7", you'll have ample marginal area and blank reverse sides for your notes, directions, sketches, etc.

2. Make notes in the margins and on the blank reverse sides regarding:

Tone and mood you want developed in each scene.
Stage business.            } A helpful hint follows
Movement of the actors.  } in the next paragraph.

# 20 DAY PRODUCTION CALENDAR

| 1 | 2 | 3 | 4 | 5 |
|---|---|---|---|---|
| | CASTING | ANNOUNCEMENT OF CAST RECRUITMENT OF PRODUCTION STAFF | RECRUITMENT OF STAFF CONTINUED WORK ON DIRECTOR'S BOOK | REHEARSAL #1 "READ-THRU" |

| 6 | 7 | 8 | 9 | 10 |
|---|---|---|---|---|
| R#2 "WALK-THRU" | R#3 PROJECTION TESTS | R#4 FROM BEGINNING OF PLAY, USING HAND PROPS | R#5 | R#6 NO SCRIPTS PROMPTER ON SET |

| 11 | 12 | 13 | 14 | 15 |
|---|---|---|---|---|
| R#7 | R#8 | R#9 | R#10 | R#11 |

EMPHASIS ON CHARACTERIZATION, DICTION, TIMING AND SPECIFIC SCRIPT PROBLEMS

| 16 | 17 | 18 | 19 | 20 |
|---|---|---|---|---|
| R#12 "RUN-THRU" | R#13 DOVETAILING OF ACTOR'S AND STAGE CREW'S EFFORTS | R#14 PRE-DRESS REHEARSAL | R#15 DRESS REHEARSAL | PERFORMANCE |

Figure 3-1

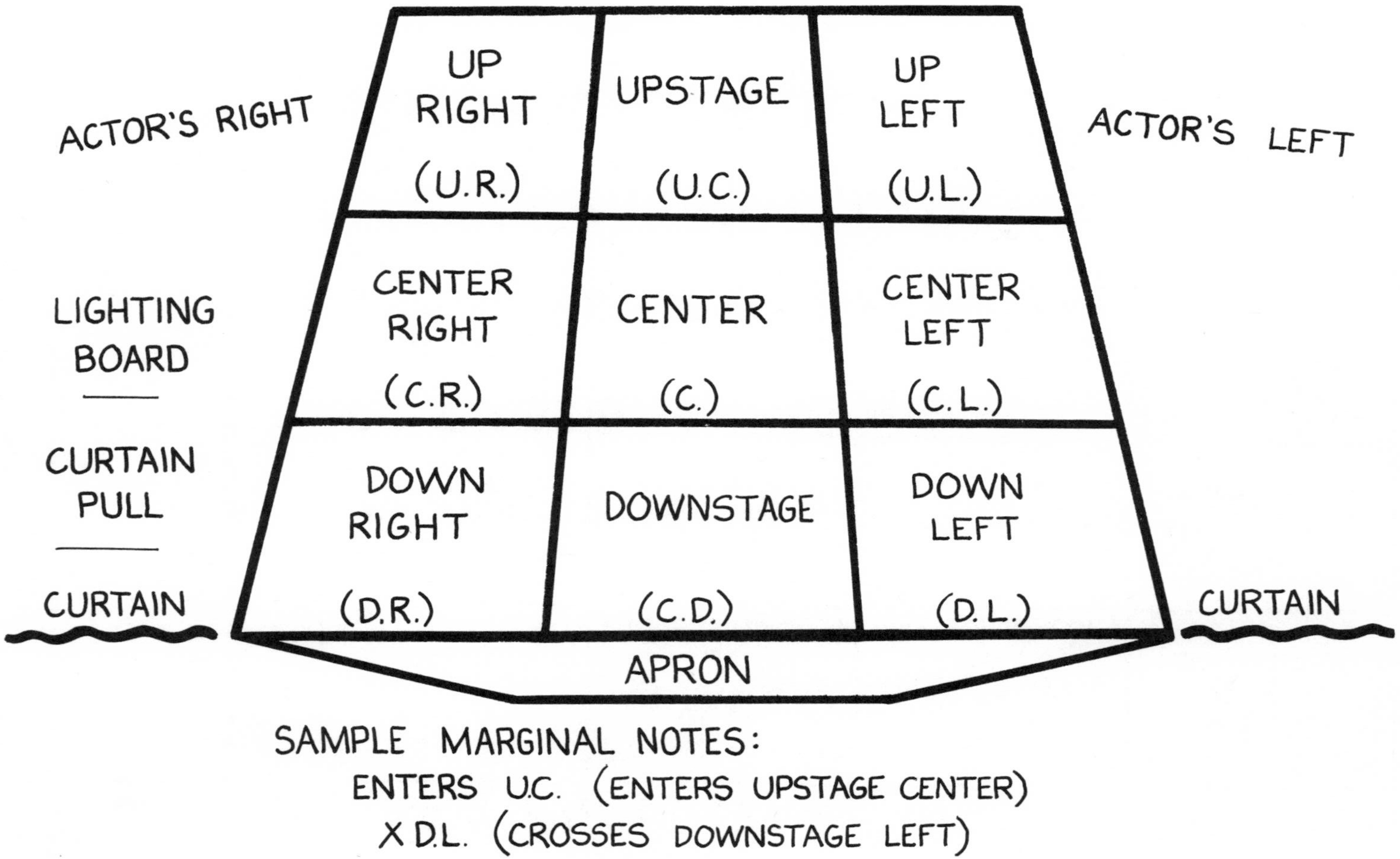

ACTOR'S LEFT

| UP LEFT (U.L.) | UPSTAGE (U.C.) | UP RIGHT (U.R.) |
| CENTER LEFT (C.L.) | CENTER (C.) | CENTER RIGHT (C.R.) |
| DOWN LEFT (D.L.) | DOWNSTAGE (C.D.) | DOWN RIGHT (D.R.) |

APRON

CURTAIN

ACTOR'S RIGHT

LIGHTING BOARD
___

CURTAIN PULL
___

CURTAIN

SAMPLE MARGINAL NOTES:
ENTERS U.C. (ENTERS UPSTAGE CENTER)
X D.L. (CROSSES DOWNSTAGE LEFT)

Figure 3-2

40

**ONE MAN IN HIS TIME**

*Sits ② ms. + acct.*
*book in hands*

HEMINGE: Are you leaving so directly?

SHAKESPEARE:  Tomorrow.  (*Raising voice*) Samuel, here's tuppence to buy the supper both you and Kit missed tonight.

*Tosses coin to*
*Samuel*

SAMUEL: Thank you sir.  Come, Kit. We will be off for supper. (*Short pause*)

*Samuel and Kit*
*exit; their footsteps*
*recede on stairs.*
*W.S. × to window*
*to look out and*
*down. Burbage*
*faces mirror UR,*
*acts out a greeting,*
*sweeps off hat,*
*bows, adjusts*
*hat, smiles, turns C,*
*well pleased*

BURBAGE: Now, let's to business. ←

*B. moves stool CR,*
*sits half-facing W.S.*
*Opens acct. book*
*Speaks sharply*

HEMINGE: Will may like to hear this financial report. Will! What do you find outside that window of more interest than the takings on our July tour?

SHAKESPEARE: I was watching Kit striding alongside Samuel, watching and wondering.  They're gone now. What of our finances?  How have we been faring? ←

*Shakes head in*
*puzzlement.  ×  to*
*Heminge's R*
*Listens carefully*

HEMINGE: Fair.    Bath, 30 shillings; Shrewsbury, 20; Coventry, 40; Ipswich, 25; Oxford, 40.

SHAKESPEARE: I call that good for a summer tour in country towns. ←

*×C; nods with*
*satisfaction*

*Leaps to feet;*
*× to CR of W.S.*

BURBAGE: Enough about money. Now, Will, the new play that you brought from Stratford — it has a fat part for me, of course.

*Puts hand on W.S.'s*
*shoulder*

SHAKESPEARE (*Laughing*): Aye, a fat part, of course.  It is you who draw the audiences, Dick. ←

*Grasps B's arm*

*Suddenly modest*

BURBAGE: Hm-m-m. . . . I can fairly claim that I bring them in, but many come to see any new play Shakespeare has done.   What's the new title?

**Figure 3-3**

Specific line and character interpretations with pauses.
   timing, etc.
Special effects (for example, an explosion offstage—
   large pan lids banged together).
Lighting effects (for example, "smoke" from fireplace—
   dry ice dropped into a pan of water).

Simplify your note-making on stage business and the movement of the actors by familiarizing yourself with the symbols traditionally used to indicate the acting areas of the stage. You'll understand the stage diagram below more easily if you stand facing the audience in the center (c) of the stage you'll be using. The stage space to your right is stage right (R), and the space to your left is stage left (L). Behind you to the back wall is upstage (U), and in front of you toward the audience is downstage (D) (Figure 3-2).

Figure 3-3 shows a sample page from a director's book.

The excerpt is from the play, *One Man in His Time* by Grace A Mayr, reprinted by permission from *Plays, The Drama Magazine for Young People.*

3. Include costume designs and descriptions, particularly if you're doing a period play, and add make-up notes.

4. Draw up a list of properties needed and a sketch of the floor plan of the setting for the property manager.

For example, your play is a mystery whose plot is based on the unexplained disappearance of Heidi Strang, a foreign travel agent. This might be the floor plan of the setting, Heidi's garden-apartment living room:

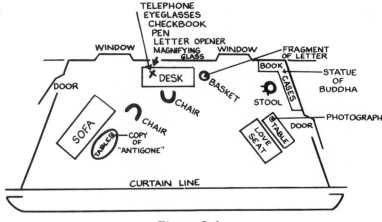

**Figure 3-4**

And here's a list of the necessary props in order of their use for the property manager:

— Copy of the Greek tragedy "Antigone" on coffee table.

— Photograph of Heidi and an older man on the table behind the love seat.

— Torn fragment of a letter in the basket L of desk.

— Telephone, eyeglasses, a checkbook, a pen, a letter opener, a magnifying glass on the writing surface of the desk.

— A Buddha, large enough to screen from view the packet of letters hidden behind it on top of the bookcase, L wall.

5. Work out the lighting and special effects schedules. (See Chapters 7 and 10.)

6. List the names and telephone numbers of parents who have agreed to help with costumes, make-up, transportation (for example, driving cast and crew to present a preview advertisement in another school.)

7. Add anything else that you feel will help you personally to direct your production staff, whatever its size and complexity.

## SUGGESTED PERSONNEL FOR THE SMALL PRODUCTION STAFF (for 10-18 Minute Play Performed by Actors, Ages five to eight)

A minimal production staff will competently serve for a 10-18 minute play with actors ages five to eight. You need another capable teacher, a willing parent or two and the school custodian. The custodian is quite the most valuable assistant any director can find, for he knows what's in every nook and cranny of his "plant" and how to get it if you need it, knows how to operate every piece of school equipment and usually how to repair it, knows (and likes) his school's staff and the pupils as well as you do—in all, he's the play director's best friend. And if your play is exclusively for children, you can even forget programs. Children aren't interested in names and printed facts on a piece of paper. A program to them is just so much paper to be torn to bits, folded into an airplane, or wadded into a ball to bounce off another kid's head—before the play begins. Instead, imitate the master William Shakespeare, who used no programs. Begin the play with a prologue where an announcer (one of the cast, another child in costume or you) welcomes the audience, names the players, and explains whatever else the children should know for their greatest enjoyment of the play.

## THE LARGER PRODUCTION STAFF
### (for Play Staged by Juniors or Young Adults)
## WITH ILLUSTRATIVE ORGANIZATIONAL CHARTS AND FULL JOB DESCRIPTION FOR EACH MEMBER OF BACKSTAGE CREW AND FRONT-OF-HOUSE STAFF

A more complex organizational plan is required for productions with juniors and young adults where admission is to be charged and the public invited. From the following charts and job descriptions (with suggested sources of personnel in parentheses), select the staff that fits your special production needs.

Putting on a play is a creative-group act and demands intelligent collaboration of not only willing, but also skilled workers.

DIRECTOR: is the overall boss who has the last word in all production decisions.

BACKSTAGE CREW: handles scenery, properties, costumes, make-up, prompting, light and sound and special effects.

CAST: acts out the play.

FRONT-OF-HOUSE STAFF: handles the business management of the production.

STAGE MANAGER (manual arts teacher or high school pupil): is in charge of stage hands (pupils), who set the stage, shift and change scenery, open and close the curtain. The stage manager supervises all backstage crew members at dress rehearsals and during the performance.

PROPERTY MANAGER (capable teacher-friend or high school pupil): directs the property crew (pupils), that collects or makes, and is responsible for the safe-keeping of the stage properties (telephone, mantel clock, oil painting) and the hand properties (tennis racket, knitting, attache case—all needed by individual actors from rehearsal #4 on). The list of properties is one of the essential items in the director's book, and a copy is given to the property manager.

**Figure 3-5**

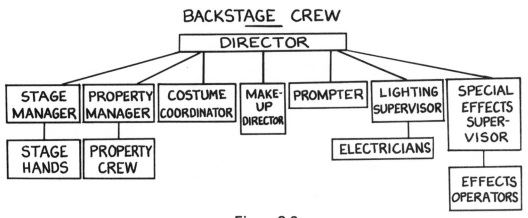

**Figure 3-6**

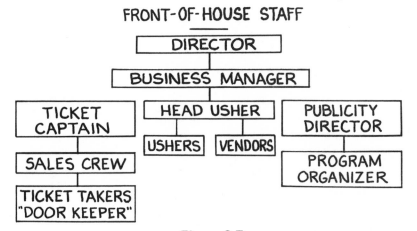

**Figure 3-7**

COSTUME COORDINATOR (home economics teacher): is in charge of costumes—assembling parts and altering them to fit, making garments or assigning and checking on their creation by volunteer pupils and adults (parents usually), supervising the rental of costumes and parts (for example, wigs) and assuming responsibility for their care, storage (there's often a good-sized clothing closet in the home economics suite), and their return in good condition after the performance.

MAKE-UP DIRECTOR (fine arts teacher or interested parent): supervises the make-up of the actors at both dress rehearsals and at the performance. The make-up director keeps the make-up box stocked and in order, arranges that a table to hold the box, a mirror, and a chair for the actor are in the make-up room, applies the make-up, and instructs the actors on make-up removal after the performance. Note: Principles of applying make-up for use under the glare of stage lights are quickly mastered by intelligent and imaginative experimentation with different shades of make-up under varied intensity and colors of lights. The test of effective stage make-up, it must be remembered, is how it looks out front.

PROMPTER (congenial co-worker): is the other staff member, besides yourself, who is in possession of an annotated copy of the playscript, plus a copy of the crew's cue sheets, and whose duties include prompting the actors in their lines and monitoring the backstage operators of light, sound and special effects at dress rehearsals and at the performance. The prompter also may be expected to pinch-hit for the director in an emergency by conducting a rehearsal "by the book"—the prompter's book—and is the logical staff member to "check-in" the actors as they arrive for dress rehearsals and the performance.

**Clear Directions for the Make-Up of the Prompter's Book**

Although this prompter's book is by no means as fat with notes and sketches and lists as the director's book, its physical format is the same. The director ought to assume responsibility for making it up, but the prompter adds all the notations, following the coaching of the actors by the director.

If the script is typed, follow the same procedure of locking the pages into a loose-leaf binder, as used for your director's book. If the script is in a printed playbook, use two copies and follow the procedure of mounting the pages described in the directions for the director's book.

Since the prompter sits in on rehearsals #6 through #15, the prompt book will have the prompter's own notes on directions for stage business and the places in the script and the length of pauses. (The prompter certainly doesn't want to rush in with cues to upset an actor who's in full control of his lines.) At rehearsals #14 and #15 and at the performance, the prompter sits in the wings near the lighting board with the prompt book and all lighting, sound and special effects cue sheet schedules in hand to help synchronize the work of the crew and the players.

LIGHTING SUPERVISOR (school custodian or high school pupil): is in charge of the lighting board and the board electricians (pupils), who follow the lighting cue sheet supplied by the director.

SPECIAL EFFECTS SUPERVISOR (music director or high school pupil): has the job of creating and directing effects to be produced by special effects operators (pupils) with sound equipment such as recordings or tapes, or with any other mechanical device for effects like the ringing of a telephone, snow falling past a window, the blowing of a police whistle or the rumble of thunder. Also, he or she may need to use other means for special effects like an offstage scream or the thud of a falling body.

BUSINESS MANAGER (mathematics or business management teacher): keeps all financial records such as ticket printing costs, sales proceeds, royalty fees, costume rentals, costs of construction materials for scenery, costumes, properties and fees paid for security officers at performance, and supervises a staff of assistants (pupils)—the ticket captain, sales crew, ticket takers, head ushers, usher corps, vendors, publicity director and the program organizer.

TICKET CAPTAIN (high school pupil): heads the ticket sales crew. The tickets are designed by the director or the business manager with the help of a commercial printer or the print shop teacher, and the printing of the tickets is ordered with a delivery date at least two weeks prior to the performance, to allow ample time for sales. A small prize such as complimentary tickets or the fun of being "doorkeeper," (the main ticket taker at the performance) will provide a good incentive to spark the sales crew. The ticket captain assigns ticket packets to the sales people, checks regularly on sales progress, and reports and deposits all ticket money with the business manager as it comes in. On the occasion of the performance, the ticket captain occupies the "box office"—a table and a chair set conveniently near the main entrance for sale of tickets.

HEAD USHER (pupil): organizes the corps of ushers and vendors and supervises their activities before and after the performance and during the intermission.

USHER CORPS: are pupils who are willing to dress in some fairly uniform fashion for easy identification; for example, dark slacks and white tops or, perhaps, long-skirted dresses with hair flowers for girls, if the corps agrees and the director approves. Their duties are to distribute programs, usher guests to seats, answer questions about curtain time and the location of toilet facilities, and to be generally helpful.

VENDORS: are staff members only in so far as they are answerable to the head usher. Usually the vendors sell their wares on trays or at a table in the lobby during intermission, the proceeds going wholly to the benefit of the school group they represent (e.g., a service club or a sports boosters club).

PUBLICITY DIRECTOR (high school pupil with talent for writing, possibly a reporter for the school newspaper): promotes ticket sales, publicizes the play, and assists the program organizer if any acknowledgment and thanks for help with the production are to be included on the program. The publicity director is the only member of the Front-of-the-House staff who must read the play, attend a rehearsal or two, and know the production personnel well enough to publicize the play with original and imaginative ideas.

### Five Channels for Good Publicity—Newspapers, Posters, Previews, Flyers, Radio and TV

1. *Newspapers*—Short press releases with attention-getting headlines covering the various aspects of the production. A press release should be typed on one side of one sheet, 8½" x 11", double-spaced with wide margins and should give the *who* (cast and production staff), *what* (title and author of play), *when* (performance date and curtain time), *where* (place of performance) and *why* (reason for play—a benefit performance for the ball teams or the scholarship fund or the senior class trip, perhaps). The more names mentioned the better. Newspapers are in business; names and faces sell copies.

Accompanying pictures (glossy prints) of a scene or two from the play are especially welcome.

The deadline set by a newspaper editor for the submission of publicity copy like this is sacrosanct. If a newspaper publishes only once a week, meeting its deadline is all the more important because missing it means losing out on publicity for a full week.

If the copy submitted has been earmarked with a request for release on a specific date, but fails to appear, an immediate follow-up with the editor will usually reveal the reason—maybe, a missed deadline or the submission of a carbon instead of an original copy (both serious errors on the part of any publicity director). On the other hand, the copy submitted may have been misplaced and a prompt checkup will take care of the problem.

The school newspaper is also a fine medium for advertisement of the play if it publishes within the four weeks prior to the performance.

2. *Posters*—The fine arts classes, with the encouragement of the art teacher (whom you have no doubt had the excellent foresight to invite to serve on the production staff in an advisory capacity at least) will usually turn out a number of eye-catching posters. If not, the publicity director may have to settle for less artistic posters made with the help of volunteers—some of the actors in minor roles, perhaps. Some strategic locations for posters are:

— Busy spots around school such as the cafeteria, main hall, library, principal's office, guidance office.
— Store windows on the main shopping street in town.
— Public library bulletin board.
— Bulletin board at most supermarket checkouts.

3. *Previews*—A short provocative scene (five to seven minutes playing time) from the play, staged at an assembly program as an announcement-advertisement, whips up interest among the student body. If this publicity ploy is well-received, get permission through your principal to stage the scene in other schools in town, maybe in neighboring towns too. This experience will give the actors and the crew who go with them exposure to audience reaction. It will also establish a friendly rapport with other schools.

4. *Flyers*—A handbill duplicated inexpensively on colored paper which announces the coming attraction is a surefire attention-getter if the flyers are distributed downtown along Main Street and

at other principal shopping areas on the Saturday afternoon just preceding the performance by the *actors themselves* with individual invitations, like "Come see me in   Name of play   on Date of performance.  I'll blow you a kiss on my curtain call."

5. *Radio and TV*–Some local stations cooperate with educational institutions by making spot announcements over the air of fund-raising events like a flea market, a carnival, a ball game, a play, even a cake sale.  A telephone call to the program director of the station with a request for coverage may result in the widest publicity possible.  In the metropolitan area of New York City, radio station WOR has often rendered this valuable service.

## Two Imaginative Publicity Stunts

Two livelier and more original supplementary approaches are:

1.  The use of car stickers or bumper placards.  These can be turned out by the school print shop, commercially printed (they're not that costly) or handmade, and distributed for display two weeks before the performance.

2.  The display in a local supermarket parking lot on Saturday afternoon just before the performance, when the actors are distributing flyers, of a decorated truck or station wagon bearing large placards announcing the performance.  Taped music will draw attention and a crowd.  Permission for this one must be obtained from the supermarket manager and from the police.

No doubt your publicity director will be nimble-witted enough to suggest more imaginative stunts for your approval.

PROGRAM ORGANIZER (high school pupil skilled in the language arts, especially meticulous in spelling all those names and titles that must appear on programs):  prepares the program copy and arranges for its duplication.

## Make-Up of Programs

The program, the playbill, duplicated on school office machines or printed, can be as simple or as elaborate as the occasion demands as long as these seven items appear with all names spelled correctly. (Wasn't it Florenz Ziegfeld who said, "Say anything you like about me, just spell my name right"?)

1. Title and author of the play.

2. Name of the group presenting the play.

3. Cast in order of appearance with the names of the actors.

4. Time and place of the presentation.

5. Names of production staff with titles, including the director, backstage crew and the front-of-house staff.

6. Generous acknowledgment of credit and thanks to people who have provided services, costumes, properties for the production (for example, acknowledgment to the local store that has loaned furniture for stage props.)

7. Names of patrons, if the production has been so sponsored.

**Three Timely Tips for You Only**

1. If paid advertisements of local merchants are to appear in the program, be sure the ad copy is submitted to each merchant for approval before you authorize printing or duplication of the program copy.

2. If musical selections such as an overture, entr'acte selections, and solo numbers (all of which enhance the artistic appeal and entertainment value of any dramatic production, to say nothing about the broader potential here for the sale of tickets to friends and relatives of the musicians) are to be included on the program, consult with the school's music director and choose selections and performers that best sustain the mood and the tone of your play.

3. As a gracious gesture, send complimentary tickets to the local government officials, the members of the Board of Education, your principal, your superintendent and any other people whose support of the school drama program you wish to recognize.

**Let's Review:**

Plan well in advance with your director's book with its sketch of the set; costume designs; copy of the script and its properties, lighting, sound, special effects lists, and its annotations in the margins for action, stage business, line and character interpretation.

Choose compatible and enthusiastic people you can work with happily for your production staff, and then give them and their roles in the production as much attention as you give the cast. They are equally important to the success of the play.

A last word to you before rehearsals start:

There are hours of fun and hard work ahead. You'll need

great physical stamina to survive the large expenditure of energy that will be demanded of you. You'll need understanding and tact to handle all the complexities of personality interreactions that will arise with so many people working closely together on a creative group project. You'll need the grace to accept equitably both the praise and the criticism that are inevitably the lot of the director.

And so—let the rehearsals begin!

# CHAPTER 4

# Dynamic Plans to Carry You from Read-Through to Dress Rehearsal

Here *you*, the director, are the star performer. Like a magician, you will now transform a script of mere words, static black on white, to a moving and spirited stage play—all in 15 rehearsals, and with no hocus-pocus!

## THE READ-THROUGH

### Rehearsal #1

With your director's book under your arm, copies of the script and the rehearsal schedule in hand, you are ready. This first rehearsal calls for the entire cast to sit in a semicircle and read the play aloud.

Follow these five no-fail steps:

1. Distribute scripts.

2. Give the theme of the play, its tone (light comedy, tragedy, melodrama) and thumbnail sketches of the characters and their costumes.

3. Have the play read aloud by the actors, with you reading stage directions. A one-act play reads in 20-25 minutes; a three-act play, in a little over an hour.

4. Present the rehearsal schedule for discussion and, at this time, allow any actor to be excused from a specific rehearsal if he or she has a bona fide prior commitment; for example, a dentist's or

doctor's appointment, or a private music lesson. Use your own judgment.

Then make three points clear:

*First,* that the schedule shall be adhered to strictly—by you as well as the cast.

*Second,* that each actor must attend rehearsals faithfully and promptly.

*Third,* that any actor who persists in inexcusable tardiness and/or absence will be replaced.

Emphasize these three points for upper-school productions, where most rehearsals have to be scheduled in free time after school. For the younger cast in lower grades, when the teacher-director spends most of the school day with the same group of children, rehearsals can be, and preferably are, scheduled during school hours. A read-through is rehearsal #1 in this case also.

Decide with the cast where the rehearsal schedule shall be posted for easy reference; for example, the main corridor or the director's classroom bulletin board. Next advise them of the measures that will be taken if any actor fails to maintain this schedule:

1—2—3 and Out

1. Reprimand for first offense (tardiness and/or absence).
2. Warning of replacement for second offense.
3. Replacement, using the runner-up for the part when roles were first cast, for persistent tardiness and/or absence.

You must exercise your director's right to hold the cast to the rehearsal schedule because allowing an actor, no matter how good an actor he or she is, to get away with wasting rehearsal time will have a harmful effect on this actor as well as on the spirit of the rest of the cast.

5. Solve with the cast any script problems, like profanity, smoking, drinking or love scenes, and direct the actors to write in changes or deletions in their own scripts.

**Happy Solutions to Four Script Problems**

*Profanity* can always be watered down to inoffensive expletives.

*Smoking* usually can be eliminated; if not, it's easy to handle.

Father is a pipe-smoker, eh? It's part of his characterization, so he "smokes." He "fills" his pipe with pinched fingers holding imaginary tobacco from his humidor, tamps it down expertly. He strikes a match and assumes the proper facial contortions of sucked-in cheeks. Ah, contentment suffuses his face. He blows out the match. Now he "smokes"—he grips the pipe between his teeth and puffs outward, sending skyward a feather of smoke, a plume of talcum powder previously loaded into the bowl. This works especially well in historical plays where Indians and colonists pass the peace pipe.

OR—Father uses the pipe (with empty bowl) as a hand prop. He grips it between his teeth, bowl upside down. He gestures with it, pointing at an object or a person, but he never smokes it. If necessary, write in a covering line: *Had to give up tobacco for my health, but I won't give up the pipe.*

OR—If the script calls for a cigarette or a cigar to be smoked, the only answer (since school and many public-hall fire laws prohibit any other solution) is to have the character pick up the cigarette or cigar, start to strike the match, but instead visibly register on his or her face some change of mind that involves other stage business. Done in character, this solution often improves the pacing of the scene.

*Drinking,* taboo for the most part, may be permitted if disapproval of it is implied. (The drinking character must come to a bad end.) No problem here, really, for it must be generally known by this time that all the drinking done by professionals in the movies, on TV, and on the stage is faked. What everyone is drinking is cold tea or water.

*Love Scenes* are best played lightly, tempered with the good judgment of both actors and director. Generally amateurs, particularly the males, are glad enough to skip love scenes entirely. This is a great pity because, properly handled, a love scene adds zest as well as romantic sparkle to any production. Minor demonstrations of affection, like holding hands, a quick embrace, a peck on the cheek, can be handled gracefully, but for most school-age actors serious love scenes are embarrassing to play in public, and distressingly funny for the audience.

This is how one director salvaged a love scene disaster: The high-spirited hero determined for a kiss was to chase and catch the reluctant heroine, but when the two played out the scene they were so awkward in their efforts that they knew the results were ludicrous.

"What would you do," the director asked the girl, "if this happened to you in real life?"

"If I really didn't want him to kiss me," the girl said, bobbing her head emphatically, "I'd whirl around on him, push him away hard, and say, 'Don't you dare!' and I'd mean it!"

And that's how the scene was played to the satisfaction of everyone, particularly the panting hero, who hadn't quite figured out how to handle a running kiss in either real life or stage acting. The answer to problems with love scenes you want to keep is to *Improvise.*

The actors may also have some good ideas about updating the language of the play or its jokes, if the play is modern but over 10 years old. Deletions and changes are accepted more readily by the actors when they've had a hand in making them. With most scripts for lower grades these problems do not exist. If anything in the original script might offend local mores, why not delete or alter the lines, the action or the character before the scripts are distributed to the young players? If a character cannot be written out of the play, alter the race, sex, age or whatever is offensive in the controversial character, supplying covering lines to fill in the resultant break in the line of action.

## THE WALK-THROUGH

**Rehearsal #2**

*Place*—School auditorium.

*Characters*—Cast and director.

*Setting*—Bare stage except for portable blackboard on which is chalked the stage floor plan for the play, showing placement of furniture on the set, location of windows and doors, positions of essential stage props, like a telephone, a fireplace, etc.

*Lighting*—Overheads only.

*Opening Scene*—The director, director's book in hand, stands before the blackboard, chalking in the moves of the players. The cast, each with script and pencil, listens and pencils in directions, and notes hand props, which are to be used at every rehearsal from now on. This is called *blocking out the play*, letting the actors know where they're supposed to be at specific times so they won't be bumping into each other on stage.

Now let's assume you're doing the kind of play most popular with young amateurs—a contemporary light comedy with one set (a living room); 10-12 actors (more or less evenly divided between males and females); with no special lighting effects beyond overheads, footlights and maybe a baby spot; no tricky sound effects, except perhaps background music, the ringing of a telephone or doorbell, the offstage shound of rain, thunder or of a falling object. You've worked on the blocking out ahead of time. It's all in your director's book. It's just a matter of chalking in the moves on the blackboard and/or delineating areas on the stage floor. Do not use chalk on the floor! Remember, the relationship of trust and cooperation you need to establish and maintain with the custodial staff, who can be immeasurably helpful if they are sympathetic to the project! Use masking tape, and have the actors remove it at the end of the rehearsal.

After the actors have made their notes, set the stage using rough approximations for the furniture and stage props (e.g., two or three chairs for a sofa, a paper carton for the telephone table). Now comes the walk-through of the play, the actors following your blocking out of the action and you supplying a running condensation of the lines while they do it. At the end of the walk-through (again you've kept it as short a rehearsal as possible, certainly within the allotted time on the rehearsal schedule) dismiss the cast with instructions to memorize their parts as quickly as possible. Four rehearsals from now, at rehearsal #6, actors may not use scripts on stage.

## THREE EARLY REHEARSALS EMPHASIZING EFFICIENT VOICE PROJECTION AND THE USE OF HAND PROPS

### Rehearsals #3—#5

These three rehearsals follow as scheduled. Now you're beginning to work on the acting. Start the third rehearsal with the projection test. It may take the entire session to test each actor's ability to project (throw forward) his voice so every word can be heard by the back row and balcony audience.

Post some members of the cast at the rear of the house, in the far corners and in the balcony. In turn, ask each actor to speak his most important speech from center stage behind the curtain line (See stage chart) and ask the listeners to report on audibility. As one actor succeeds; that is, opens his mouth sufficiently and articulates clearly enough to be heard easily, test another actor.

It's best for you to remain on stage for two reasons:

1. Peer criticism wins readier response.

2. On stage you're there to demonstrate what you want the actor to do. You can show that being heard does not depend on horrific mouthing of the words nor on raucous shouting, but upon throwing the voice forward in a natural effort to be heard.

Teach the actors to open their mouths wide so that the sound comes out smoothly in loud tones.

The actors may feel they're shouting and that their voices bounce off the walls of the auditorium in echoes. Tell them that when the house is full at the performance there will be no echoes and no apparent shouting, only clearly heard, well-projected lines. This has to do with acoustics. Because an audience forms a highly absorptive surface, sound waves that touch the listeners are much reduced in strength.

Tell them that if the performance were to be held outdoors, the actors would have to double, even triple their efforts to be heard. Tell them that in the outdoor amphitheatre of ancient Greece, actors used megaphones fashioned into their open-mouthed masks as voice amplifers.

If one of your actors has trouble projecting his voice, assign to that actor a partner, a minor member of the cast to be a listener and critic until the problem is solved. If you yourself need to rehearse an actor alone, encourage that actor to think the lines through and then say them in particular to that fellow in the last row in the balcony who is falling asleep with boredom.

An actor may fluff his lines, may fall flat on his face, may even miss an entrance cue—all is forgiven and the audience still loves him, but let him mumble his lines so he cannot be heard and the audience hates him. The audience has come to listen as well as to see (*Audio*—Latin for *I hear* is the origin of the word—the cast should remember this).

Believe me, every last one of them can project a voice and be heard. They've been doing it since they were bawling infants, screaming nightly for attention from their day-worn parents who were seeking some peace and quiet; or kindergartners, proclaiming sand-box rights; or upper-schoolers, cheering their ball teams in Little League; etc.

This projection test may take up all of Rehearsal #3.  No matter, it's time well spent.

At Rehearsal #4, start at the beginning of the play and rehearse the actors and make comments and corrections.  Remember, they should be using hand props—tennis racket, guitar, book, spectacles, or knitting needles. Stress the line of action of the play and how each character contributes to the suspense or rising interest to the climax of the play.  Go as far as possible in the play, but terminate the rehearsal on time.

At Rehearsal #5 pick up where Rehearsal #4 left off.  Don't start over every time, or you'll find you've over-rehearsed the opening and never done justice to the middle or the end of the play.  Remind the cast to bring all hand props again next time, but no scripts onto the set.  No serious coaching can be achieved until the actors know their lines.  What you don't tell them is that next time, the person, who in time probably will know the play as well as you do and who can take over a rehearsal if need be, will be present—the prompter.

### Your Stand-in—the Prompter

The prompter is a competent and reliable member of the production staff, whose job is to be ever-present backstage, ready to prompt the actors when they forget their lines, and to cue the sound and light effects people backstage at the time of the dress rehearsal and the final performance.

In a high school production, the prompter can be a reliable student, one of the understudies, or another interested teacher.  In the lower school production, the prompter could be an aide, another teacher on the teaching team, or a colleague for whom you can return the favor.

This prompter, really your assistant in coaching the actors, will have a book—a large notebook containing the script with marginal notes of your acting instructions and line interpretations, including pauses (especially pauses) so the prompter won't be spoiling a dramatic effect at a long "pregnant pause" by hurling lines at an actor.  The prompter will know the play inside out by curtain time and could probably pinch-hit for you at some of the later rehearsals, coaching from the book.

A prompter grown sensitive to the actors' work after a period of sitting in on rehearsals recognizes the panicky faltering of an actor groping for lines and feeds in a phrase or two until the actor is back to normal.

Good prompting never is audible to the audience, of course, for the prompter, the backbone of the production, is definitely a backstage figure. There's a stage tradition, pooh-poohed by many serious students of the theatre, that William Shakespeare started his spectacular stage career this way as book-holder (prompter) for the Burbage Theatre on the outskirts of London back in the 1580s. From prompter to playwright may be not so long a jump at that!

## FIRST REHEARSAL WITHOUT SCRIPTS

### Rehearsal #6

*Place*—preferably the stage in the school auditorium, but any cleared floor space with improvised furniture and stage props will do.

*Characters*—actors without scripts, but with all hand props (letter for heroine, transistor radio for her kid brother, knitting for grandma), the prompter off in the wings (permanent offstage position) and the director.

Now for a run-through of the play without coaching from opening scene to curtain, which may carry over to the next rehearsal, depending on the length of the play. Insist, however, that actors face the audience as much as possible when they speak and are careful not to block one another from the audience's line of vision.

This run-through without coaching gives the actors a chance to demonstrate their mastery of their lines, to use their hand props, and to learn the location of the prompter. Note: A good idea for an actor who is floundering for lines is to gravitate slowly and naturally across the stage toward the prompter in the wings so the lines come through in tones audible only to the actor.

Very early on in rehearsals the actors must accustom themselves to using their hand props and wearing anything especially tricky to manipulate, like a sword (Oh, can that be a wayward accessory when the actor sits down or even walks!), a hoop skirt (Oops! Watch sitting down in this or backing up too suddenly against a wall or sofa!), a mask (hot and sound-muffling), a feathered headdress for an Indian chief (bit hard to balance at first), milady's fan, the queen's train, the king's crown, the duke's moustache, the princess's long golden wig of curls, the witch's broomstick, the farmer's pitchfork—all skillfully handled only after practice.

Don't try to do anything else at this rehearsal, except take notes yourself where special coaching on characterization, line interpretation, diction, timing, etc. is needed.

## COACHING ACTORS' SKILLS

### Rehearsals #7—#11

During the next four rehearsals devote your efforts to detailed coaching of the actors' skills. Insist that each actor on stage, speaking or not, remain in character as a part of the whole picture. (This three-sided stage most of us use is, in essence, a picture frame.) Never allow the actors to forget there's going to be an audience out there at curtain time—a paying audience perhaps, that expects and deserves its money's and its time's worth.

Here's help solving some of those problems you noted during Rehearsal #6:

### Characterization

*Problem:* Your actors are two-dimensional, like cardboard puppets, spouting lines by rote so that the drama is underplayed, dry, lifeless. What to do?

Choose a lively scene in the play and:

1. Try the extra-larger-than-life attack where each actor plays it big, shouts his lines and gestures extravagantly. The telephone rings. The heroine doesn't walk; she dashes to answer. Exaggeratedly tossing her head, she sweeps the receiver under her hair and trills a vibrating *hello.* The hero doesn't walk into the room; he strides. The flirt over-flirts, rolling eyes and hips. The villain twirls his moustache while he heh-hehs at the good guys.

Over-play! Over-do! Over-act! Over-everything! Is this any way to play a scene? Of course not! It's just a relaxing fun exercise to be used once to loosen up the inhibitions of the actors. Most of this hyperbolical over-playing wears off; some of it sticks. You do need a larger-than-life projection of character for stage acting. The use of make-up is part of it: the rouge for lips and cheeks, the dark penciling for eyebrows and age lines, which accentuate facial features for greater visibility across the footlights.

2. Using the same scene, follow #1 by the slowdown. Require actors to think through each line and its accompanying gesture before speaking. Demand their deliberate movement from one

position on stage to another position and their explanation of why each movement is necessary. When the actors know how their characters think and why they gesture and move as they do, their characterizations will improve.

Never allow your actors on stage to step out of the play mentally between speeches and simply wait for cues. Remind them that acting also means re-acting. Actors must concentrate on and react to the speeches and actions of other actors on stage, since each character is a part of the picture the audience sees. A good idea is to tell each actor to start thinking his or her part several minutes before an entrance and to maintain it until well offstage after the scene.

If an actor, even a minor character, continues having trouble interpreting a part, failing to think and feel the lines before speaking, show this actor how you see the bit done. Invent more stage business to accompany the lines. Having something to do tends to free an actor's mind somewhat for delivery of lines. Couldn't lovable old Gramps, who's having difficulty thinking sixtyish and remembering he's slow-moving and a bit arthritic, be given a cane to use and additional stage business? Have him squint to read the incriminating words on a burnt scrap of a letter he's just drawn out of the fireplace ashes with his new hand prop, the cane. He frowns, shakes his head, needs his glasses. He pantomimes a brief, fruitless search of his vest pockets and the mantelpiece. At length his face lights up, and he reaches for his glasses on top of his head, where they've been fully visible, to the amusement of the audience, the whole time. Gramps the actor senses this sympathy from the audience, which he can build up for Gramps the character, and relaxes; thereby, he performs better.

All minor characters are important to the whole play and deserve careful rehearsal, even the walk-on. Show minor characters, like Gramps, how to get the most out of their parts without "stealing the scene" from the main characters.

Often a nicely timed compliment will do more to improve the acting of a minor character than hours of rehearsal and all the additional props and stage business you can give him. With that cheerleader whose part consists of one line, "Here he comes!" to herald the entrance of a four-letter star athlete into the hall for the Sports Awards Dinner, try a compliment. Just as soon as she or he projects the voice well enough to be heard in the last row of the balcony, call out an enthusiastic *"Good! Again, please, and this time step up the emphasis on "comes", and we'll have just what we want to set the mood for the whole scene."* When she or he does as you ask, compliment the cheerleader again: *"That's it!  Good!"*

## DICTION WITH FIVE SHORTCUTS TO IMPROVED DELIVERY OF LINES

*Problem:*  Your actors know their lines, they can be heard throughout the house, but they cannot always be understood.  Voice projection is more than just being heard!  The audience deserves to understand what is being said.  William Shakespeare's advice is as sound today as when Hamlet instructed the traveling players to "Speak the speech... trippingly on the tongue."

Here are five shortcuts to improved delivery of lines:

1. Demonstrate good enunciation by reading the lines of an actor and having her or him repeat the lines after you.  If you find an actor can not pronounce a particular word with ease, stumbles every time or has a verbal block on it, change the word.  *Statistics* was the nemesis of one actor—too many *st-st's.*  Once the word was changed to the phrase *facts and figures,* the problem was solved.

2. Go over the speeches with an actor who's running out of breath and help him or her with the phrasing.  Break up the lines in suitable places where pauses for breath can be taken and have the actor mark her or his script in these places for private practice.

3. Teach all the actors to dentalize—to speak with the tongue tip touching or near the upper front teeth for certain sounds; e.g., the *th* in *thin* and *this.*  Use a very literal application of dentalizing by exaggerating the use of the tongue tip and the teeth, especially for the *d's* and *t's.*  Demonstrate and have the actors repeat lines like these:

> *T*o be or no*t t*o be: *that* is *the* question
> (Hamlet again, but actors won't mind.)

> Pe*t*er, Pe*t*er, pumpkin ea*t*er

> Beau*t*iful Soup, so rich and green,
>   Wai*t*ing in a ho*t t*ureen.

> *T*winkle, *t*winkle, li*tt*le ba*t*!
> How I won*d*er wha*t* you're a*t*!

Peter, Piper, pick*ed* a peck of pickl*ed* peppers;
A peck of pickl*ed* peppers Pe*t*er Piper pick*ed*;
If Pe*t*er Piper pick*ed* a peck of pickl*ed*  peppers,
Where's the peck of pickl*ed* peppers
Pe*t*er Piper pick*ed*?

4. Tell an actor whose lines are not clearly intelligible in all parts of the house to think, as he speaks, of his voice's reaching to the farthest corner and to the topmost balcony seat, and he'll think himself into being able to do it.

5. Recommend that each actor listen the next time he or she bites into a chilled stalk of celery for the clean, crisp sound he or she produces—the exact effect desired——crisp, sharp, precise articulation.

## Timing

Good timing is the mark of the professional.  That's why farce and melodrama, both of which young players relish, are so much better done by professionals.  Timing is the essence of both forms.

Some amateur actors have a natural sense of timing, suiting the action to the word; for example, like moving forward, hand outstretched in greeting just ahead of the line *Welcome to Melrose Village, Dr. Allen;* or picking up cues by speaking almost on top of the last word of the previous speaker.  Other amateurs acquire a sense of timing during the rehearsal process.

To improve their timing, tell all actors to start thinking their roles offstage before entering and to continue playing the roles right into the wings upon exiting.

Good timing is good theatre.  Keep your actors and crew alert to its importance.  It's a gift some have naturally, a skill some learn, but a secret some never fathom.  Your actors and crew most probably fall into the first two categories, but be prepared for the third group, who may be the salt of the earth in every other respect, but you hope are not too numerous in your play company.

Accept, however, the job of helping these few as well as you can.  The play may be *the thing,* but your job is children, so don't be such a perfectionist that you make everybody, including yourself, unhappy.  This may be the only play some of these children will ever be in.  Make this one a memory worth cherishing.

## ANSWERS TO NINE SPECIFIC SCRIPT PROBLEMS

### 1. Scream of Terror

Let's say the opening scene of a one-act mystery *The Ghost of Breckenridge Barn* calls for a scream of terror from the more easily scared of two young actors—one the heroine, eager to solve the mystery, the other, her best friend, who'll do the screaming. The two enter the barn, back center, the screamer clinging to the heroine. To create the mood, lights are dim, an eerie blue, and the actors speak in stage whispers (well projected, however, to reach all corners of the house). Something flutters in the loft; in the distance an owl hoots; suddenly thunder crashes overhead, and the clinger screams in terror. This scream doesn't simply burst from the girl's throat. It requires a build-up of energy and voice, step by step. This takes practice, following four steps every time:

1. The screamer inhales several times through the mouth (well before the scream is called for).
2. As the screamer exhales, she emits each time fuller and fuller gasps, increasing the volume, until
3. the scream literally pushes itself out naturally, the carrying power of the scream depending on the force of air.
4. After the scream, the actor yawns (behind the hand she has now clapped to her mouth, so the yawn is not seen by the audience). This yawn relaxes her throat muscles, which may otherwise become constricted.

### 2. Stage Whisper

This is not a whisper at all, but a stylized, perfectly audible rendering of lines, easily heard in all parts of the house. Much of a stage whisper is achieved by the actor's attitude, which suggests confidentiality and secrecy. The audience readily falls in with the idea that these "whispers" (sometimes asides to the audience as in Shakespeare's plays, sometimes remarks in pretended undertones to actors on stage) are not heard by certain other actors. These other actors do not react to the lines; so, of course, the audience knows they have not heard them. Once you've won their sympathy, an audience is unbelievably willing to go more than halfway in this game of make-believe. It's all part of the wonderful actor-audience relationship, which supersedes reality, suspends credibility, blessedly making all necessary allowances.

### 3. Laughing and/or Crying

A laugh isn't any farther from a sob on stage than it is in real life. The stage laugh is achieved by taking a series of short breaths and simultaneously emitting soft *ho-ha's* with each breath and between breaths. The laugher increases the volume of the voice with each succeeding *ho-ha* and inhales and exhales with increasing speed until the laugh erupts at the climactic point and sounds natural.

For a sob, the actor substitutes *oh* for *ho-ha*, and uses soft panting breaths mounting in intensity until sobs break forth. Fortunately for amateur actors registering grief, an actor may partially cover his or her face with hands or bow the head, although neither of these reactions should be permitted to obscure the actor's rendering of lines.

### 4. Dialects

Like moveable holidays, a dialect is usually adjustable to a particular actor's ability, or it's expendable. If an actor can not do the Irish dialect required of O'Rourke as the jolly innkeeper and can do a good simulation of Wolfgang Schwandorfer's German accent, change the characterization to fit the actor's skills. (This ought to be done at the first rehearsal.) If the actor has trouble approximating any dialect at all, letting the actor read the lines straight usually in no way impairs the total dramatic effect.

### 5. Waiting for Laughs

This is a matter related to timing. It's timing in reverse, in a sense. Prepare your actors for the audience's laughing where no laugh has been foreseen, as well as where a laugh is expected. Tell the actors that when a good laugh erupts on a line of dialogue:

1. to wait for the audience to enjoy its laugh, but only to the point just before they're laughed out.* In other words, cut their laugh short and pick up the dialog.

2. above all, to stay in character, in a state of suspended animation during the wait.

* *Caution to actor waiting for laugh:* Don't giggle to yourself. Don't smirk at the cleverness of the line. You'd better keep a straight face, or the audience will stop laughing altogether.

### 6. Crowd Scenes

If a crowd scene must be staged, keep the "crowd" small. A stage can hold just so many actors. Block out the scene as carefully as you block out the action of the rest of the play.

1. Give each actor a precise position on the stage.

2. Give each actor something to do—strain to see over some-one's shoulder, bump into another actor, apologize or snarl, wave a flag (all in character)—so the crowd does not become too static. Allow actors to create their own bits of reaction and incorporate these into the crowd scene plan in your director's book.

3. Also compose in advance all the ad-libs called for in the script. Assign the lines to individual actors.

4. Work out and rehearse this scene as fully as any other scene, particularly the entrance and exit of the crowd. For some productions the howling crowd can "come on" with a rush through the house aisles and up those steps usually found on either side of the apron of a school stage. (See stage chart.) Exits through the house, however, tend to distract the audience from the subsequent action taking place on stage.

## 7. Fainting

If a scene calls for an actor to black-out, arrange:

1. that this actor be in a sitting position, where all that is necessary is an audible sigh and a slumping of the body with the head lolling sideways, or

2. that the actor be standing close to another actor capable of supporting and "walking" the fainter to a chair.

Do not have actors fainting from a standing position. It's not only too dangerous, but also requires a professional actor to do it properly.

## 8. The Un-Rehearsal

There comes a rehearsal somewhere between #7 and #12 when you want O U T ! This rehearsal starts late. Your mood is explosive with tension. The actors forget lines. Hand props disappear. The stage crew's timing (galloping hoofbeats, striking of the clock or whatever) is off. Half the overheads and a third of the footlights are dead, and the school maintenance staff is taking its sweet time replacing bulbs. The play is falling to pieces! Soon everyone is at everyone else's throat. Halfway through the session nervous snickering and giggling take over, and the rehearsal clowns itself into a fiasco—a reversal-rehearsal. Hang in there! Guard your rising temper. Everybody, you included, obviously needs a breather. Dismiss the rehearsal calmly with as few words as possible. Believe me, at this point nobody feels good about this, but without fail the next rehearsal will more than make up for any loss of time with an extra spurt of effort and marked improvement on the part of everyone, including you. This unrehearsal is all part of putting on a play, and will be one of the "funny" memories you will laugh over later.

## 9. Ad-libbing

Although sometimes permissible for its scene-saving value, ad-libbing by an actor is frequently disconcerting to the players and crew, and should not be permitted in rehearsal nor tolerated at the performance. If an actor, however, forgets a line, can't get within hearing distance of the prompter in the wings and no one on stage is quick-witted enough to supply the line, he or she should improvise (ad-lib) an approximation of the line and hope the next speaker hasn't been thrown off too badly to pick up the script dialog.

## FIRST RUN-THROUGH FOR ACTORS

### Rehearsal #12

Run through the play with the cast from beginning to end. Interrupt the action only when necessary to smooth out rough spots—a scene played too fast, a slow pick-up of a cue, a bit of dialog that needs highlighting.

## FIRST FULL CAST AND BACKSTAGE CREW REHEARSAL

### Rehearsal #13

Call the full cast and full crew for this rehearsal, since it is designed essentially for the stage crew to synchronize the light, sound, and any special effect (for example, snow falling past a window) with the action of the players.

The crew's cue sheet, which indicates the timing of each effect, is posted near the switchboard backstage, and a copy of it is given to the prompter.

The cast, like motion picture stand-ins, walk through their parts in the play, performing and speaking key lines that serve as cues to the crew. For example; the curtain rises on the dimly lighted living room of Richard Bromley's apartment. The telephone shrills. A door key is heard turning the lock in the door, which opens to reveal a shaft of light emanating from the hallway. Richard Bromley enters, up left. He flips a wall switch to flood the set with light, revealing to the audience, but not to him, a body sprawled before the sofa on the rug, down right. The telephone stops ringing just as

Bromley picks up the receiver and finds the line dead. At that moment the doorbell buzzes. Bromley crosses left. He opens the door to two police officers. No word has been spoken, but your stage crew has been very busy. This rehearsal is for them.

Now skip to another scene where crew members need cueing; for example, the scene where you want a baby spot focused on the "body" as Bromley and the two police officers discover that the body is actually a stuffed dummy, cleverly made up to resemble Bromley's eccentric, rich Uncle George.

Some areas of the play require more work by the crew than others. Go through these areas, but essential as this rehearsal is, keep it as brief as possible so as not to tire your actors. You don't want them waiting around too long on set out of character, lest their characterizations suffer. Fortunately they are to perform in costume and make-up at rehearsal #14.

After you dismiss the cast, run the crew through their paces again, this time with the prompter reading the cues from the prompter's cue sheet.

## SEVEN-STEP PROCEDURE FOR THE
## PRE-DRESS REHEARSAL INCLUDING
## CURTAIN-CALL ROUTINE

### Rehearsal #14

Step by step, follow this procedure to cover every detail of this important rehearsal:

1. Check set and lighting and sound effect equipment with the stage crew.

2. Call cast on stage for costume and make-up check. Make any necessary additions and changes. (There are always, however, bits and pieces of costume not available until dress rehearsal.)

3. Check properties—Hand props should be ready backstage for the actors, and stage props should be in place on the set.

4. Conduct a run-through of the play from curtain opening to closing, with you sitting out front, taking notes on anything that needs more work. The crew member in charge of the curtain may need practice on his timing with the curtain, particularly its closing. The pace of the play may need stepping up. A key scene may need

to be more sharply played. A baby spot may need to be shifted slightly.

5. Rehearse the curtain calls the players will be expected to take after the performance. This is a suggested order for curtain calls:

*First call* – entire cast with principals in center, alternating male and female players as far as possible.

*Second call* – secondary actors.

*Third call* – principal actors.

*Fourth call* – entire crew, stage crew, author of script (if play is student-written), make-up artist, etc., until everyone who has had a hand in the production has had a share of the limelight.

For each curtain call, the curtain opens, the persons on stage smile and bow graciously in acknowledgment of the applause from the audience, and the curtain closes. The stagehand on the curtain will need a strong arm and will have to pop into the fourth curtain call for a share of the applause and then pop backstage again to close the curtain for the last time.

6. Hold a brief session on stage with the cast and crew to offer any suggestions you have in your notes from this run-through. Remember that after dress rehearsal it'll be too late to do anything but pull loose ends together. This is your last real chance to coach.

7. Announce that the dress rehearsal, which is to be played as if it were a performance, will start one hour after the time listed on the rehearsal schedule. In that hour the actors will get into full costume and make-up, and the crew will set the stage, take their places backstage and on the spotlights, while you will be out front, greeting the guests whose presence will give them experience with audience reaction (and incidentally will insure the maximum effort on the part of all in putting on a good show).

## DRESS REHEARSAL

### Rehearsal #15

The guests just mentioned above could be any or all of these groups:

1. Senior Citizens. Post an invitation on the bulletin board of their meeting place.

2. Relatives of the cast and the crew. From school, telephone one or two of the mothers or fathers who are available during the day and ask them to take over the inviting of other parents, of aunts, uncles, grandparents, forty-second cousins, etc. They'll come to the performance too, don't worry. They wouldn't miss it.

3. School children of suitable age groups bused in from a special school for the disabled, from an alternative education school, from a private school, from a children's home. Your principal and the guidance people will help you, may even issue the invitation, and will be on hand to help you welcome guests on arrival.

4. Any other suitable group.

As these guests arrive, during the hour before curtain time, greet them, direct them to seats, and give them programs, if available.

Check backstage that players, crew and prompter are in places. Then join the audience. If programs are not available, step onto the stage before the curtain opens and tell the audience the name of the play, its time and place, and list the characters and the players' names. Then signal the stagehand on the curtain and rejoin the audience for the preview.

At the end of the rehearsal after the invited guests have left, gather the players and crew on stage for last instructions for the performance:

1. Direct them to report one hour before curtain time for make-up and dressing.

2. Assign the prompter to checking in the players and the crew as they arrive so you'll know everyone is present.

3. Remind actors that when they are in costume and make-up they are not to wander out into the halls or lobby to see their friends, as it destroys the illusion of the play. Of course, no one may peek through the curtains at the audience.

4. End on a note of encouragement. Any corrective criticism should be limited to errors that can be easily corrected—the country girl's sunbonnet should be worn farther back on her head to reveal more facial expression; the sheriff needs to pause longer at that key point in his lines to the newspaper reporter. It's too late now for major coaching.

In truth, your coaching job is done. Now the success of the

performance rests on the foundation of all that you have done ahead of time.  You've been teaching all this while, you know—speech projection, graceful movment and poise, teamwork, interdependence between players and crew, so many things! Consider also all that you have learned about your students from this experience.  Besides all this, rehearsing this play has been fun!

### Let's Review:

1. Solve as many script problems as possible with the cast at rehearsal #1.
2. Maintain the discipline of the rehearsal schedule scrupulously.
3. Start each rehearsal where the previous one left off so that no one part of the play is over-rehearsed.
4. Give equal coaching attention to both major and minor roles.
5. Remind actors that acting includes reacting, not only when they're speaking lines but whenever they're playing a scene.
6. Make the dress rehearsal a success by inviting an audience.
7. Remember you are not only the director of the play, but also the teacher of these students, so exercise your authority accordingly.

Our next several chapters deal largely with the technical aspects of play production, showing you ways to stage your play with maximum artistry and skill.

# CHAPTER 5

# Staging the Play...
# Your Showcase for Talent

That all the world's a stage is as true today as it's always been. Anywhere—the street, the steps of a public building, a football stadium, a shopping center, the library lawn, a church basement, the town plaza, your school gymnasium or auditorium—can be a stage. The place must offer two things only: 1) space for the players to perform, and 2) space for the audience to view the play.

With these two conditions on hand, you have theatre. That word *theatre* is from the Greek word *theatron,* meaning *seeing place.*

## EVALUATING YOUR STAGING AREA

Now, your school's seeing place, the theatre stage you must direct for, may be:

1. A traditional proscenium, or picture-frame stage in your school auditorium, complete with fly and wing space, apron, and curtain. See Figure 5-1.

2. An arena stage, or theater-in-the-round (sometimes called *circus stage),* usually at floor level in the gymnasium or any big hall with a centered circular, or oval acting area, with the audience seating (folding chairs or permanent bleachers) ranged in concentric rings around it See Figure 5-2.

73

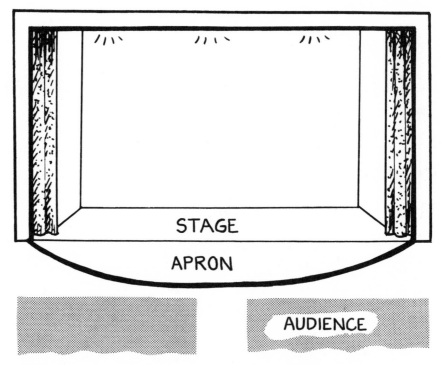

## PROSCENIUM, OR PICTURE-FRAME STAGE

Figure 5-1

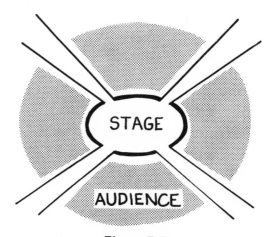

Figure 5-2

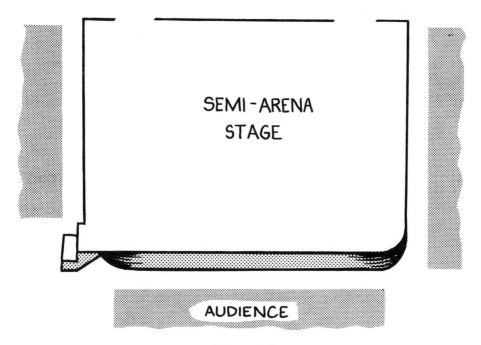

SEMI-ARENA
STAGE

AUDIENCE

**Figure 5-3**

3. A semi-arena, 3/4 arena, a thrust (or open) stage with or without a stationary raised or a movable sectioned platform. See Figure 5-3.

Directions for building this sectional stage are on page 76. This stage can be used in your gymnasium, which may also have seating in tiered balcony bleachers and floor space on three sides of the performing area for spectators. Usually the fourth side provides a scenic backing with entries for the actors.

*Note:* If your school has no auditorium, assembly hall or suitable theatre space, you may have to present your school productions elsewhere—a church hall or the town hall, for example. You may, in any case, need to rig a curtain or a cyclorama. Directions for the construction of these curtain supports follow on page 78.

Your situation may be unique. Adapt—doctor your script to the stage available to you, remembering that a script needs only players, an audience and a stage to become a play. All else—costumes, props, scenery, lighting, sound and special effects enhance, but do not make, the play.

## A SURE-FIRE PLAN FOR BUILDING
## A SIMPLE STAGE

A simple stage (which you might like to have for certain productions, even if your school is well-equipped with a more than adequate stage).

Plywood and lumber are needed for the basic structure. The plywood provides the surface on which the actors will stand and the lumber is used for the curtain supporting framework. See Figure 5-4.

This is a modular concept, so these simple stages or platforms may be easily placed side by side or in any other configuration as needed. The stage plan is 4' X 8' to accommodate the pre-cut plywood 4' X 8' sheet size.

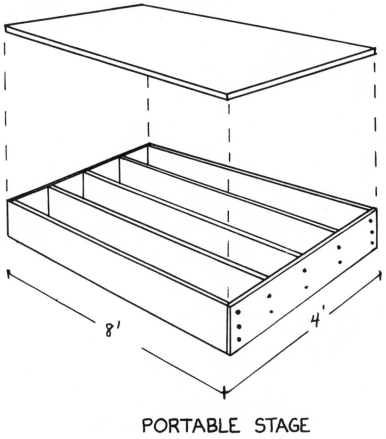

## PORTABLE STAGE
**Figure 5-4**

**You Will Need:**

Plywood 4' X 8' X 1/2" grade B interior. If the stage is to be used or stored outside, use exterior grade plywood.

Lumber 1" X 10" board (actual size is 3/4" X 9 1/4") cut to dimensions shown in Figure 5-4.

8 penny nails

2" wire brads

Covering for plywood—see following suggestions:

- Indoor-outdoor carpeting. This really is the ideal covering. It prevents the possibility of any of the performers slipping on stage.
- Linoleum or vinyl floor covering.
- Paint. Use a flat primer with a second coat of a good exterior oil paint or grey deck paint, if color is not important. This type paint has high wearing qualities.

**Procedure:**

1. Following Figure 5-4 as your design model, measure the lengths of boards needed.
2. Have your lumber dealer cut the boards to size.
3. Nail the joints, first checking for fit with right angle. Use 8 penny nails.
4. Nail the three cross members in place at 12" intervals with 8 penny nails.
5. Fasten your sheet of plywood to the frame with 2" wire brads. Place the brads at 6" intervals completely around the outside boards. To prevent squeaking, place brads at 12" intervals on the cross members.
6. Paint the framework.
7. Paint the plywood or install floor coverings, using manufacturer's instructions.

When the stage is completed, its height will be approximately 10". You may want to place a stool or make a step for the performer's easy access to the stage. Now your actors will make that step-up, rise above the floor level, and really feel like actors.

Not only do these portable stages provide basic stage units, but they can also accommodate further construction.

## A SPEEDY WAY TO BUILD A
## FRAMEWORK FOR CURTAINS

Add framework as pictured in Figure 5-5 to hold various pieces of scenery, or to support draw curtains and a cyclorama for a complete stage setting. See Figure 5-6.

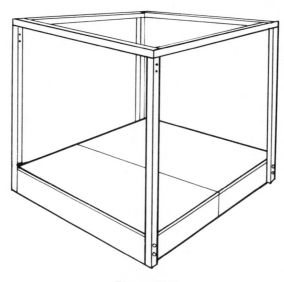

**Figure 5-5**

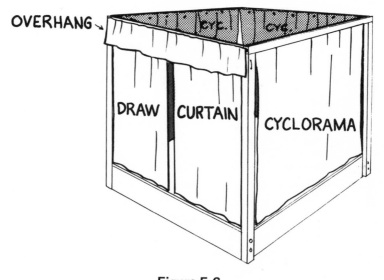

**Figure 5-6**

## You Will Need:

8 2" X 2" (1 1/2 X 1 1/2" actual size) lumber cut as follows:

> 4 pieces 8' lengths for the posts
>
> 4 pieces 8' 3" for the frame

8 penny nails

Heavy wood screws or long bolts

Drill

Saw

Paint

## Procedure:

1. Consult Figure 5-5 before working on the frame. The frame should be built before it is attached to the platform.

2. The holes for the wire supports for the draw curtains are to be drilled in two of the posts before anything else is done. The first hole will be drilled 2" from the top of the posts. The second hole will be drilled 3" from the top of the posts. See Figure 5-7.

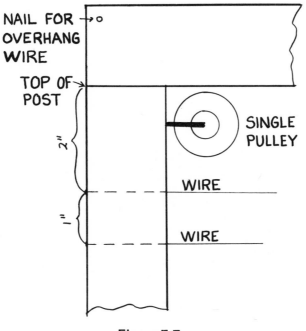

**Figure 5-7**

3. Saw a rabbet (a cut-out) on each end of the 8' 3'' boards in the dimensions shown in Figure 5-8. Two of the boards will have cuts at the top, two will have cuts at the bottom.

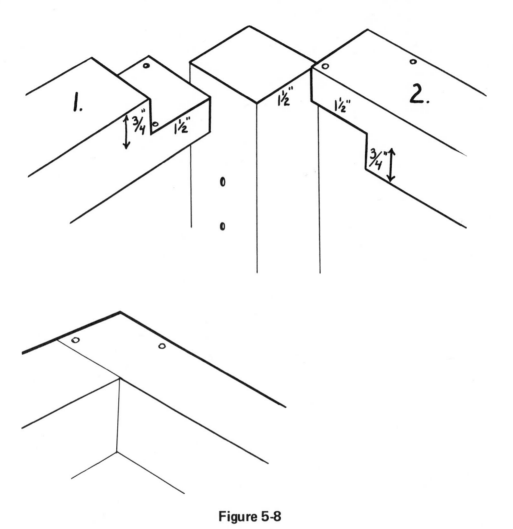

**Figure 5-8**

4. Nail the board with the top cut to the post, placing the nails in the positions shown in Figure 5-8.

5. Place the board with the opposite cuts on top of the nailed board and nail that into position.

6. After the frame is completed, with the help of the crew, bolt the posts to the stage with two long bolts or heavy wood screws.

7. Paint the curtain supporting frame to match the stage.

### ANYONE CAN INSTALL PULLEYS

**You Will Need:**

2 small awning pulleys—1 single pulley, 1 double pulley

A roll of aluminum clothesline wire

40' rope for drawing the curtain

Wood screws

**Procedure:**

1. See Figure 5-7 and fasten the pulleys with wood screws.

2. To install curtain wires; bring wire through the top holes of the posts and proceed through the bottom holes, pull taut, and twist wire ends together, tightly. See Figure 5-9.

3. After draw curtain is completed, attach rope as shown in Figure 5-9.

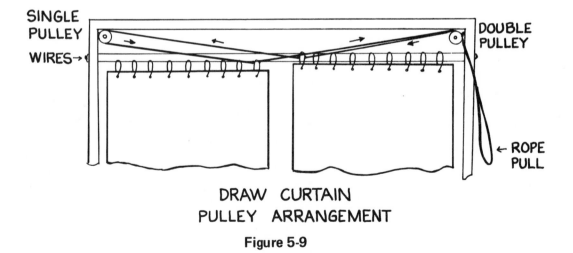

**DRAW CURTAIN
PULLEY ARRANGEMENT**

**Figure 5-9**

While your stage is being completed, work should be progressing on the draw curtains and the cyclorama (the cyc), which encloses the other three sides. However, there are openings left where the material ends at the corners and the openings can accommodate the entrance and exits of the actors. See Figure 5-6. There is also a need for a fabric overhang to cover the pulley arrangement and the top of the pull curtain's rings.

## THERE'S NO MYSTERY TO
## MAKING DRAW CURTAINS

**You Will Need:** (For a curtain to fit an 8-foot stage)

1 king-size sheet 108" X 110" OR

6-2/3 yards of 60" wide material that is light in weight, but opaque enough so the actors or crew will not be seen behind it. This material will be cut in half, making each side 3-1/3 yards long, which will allow for 3" double hems at the top and bottom.

18 grommets

18 shower curtain rings

4 weights (fishing sinkers will do nicely)

**Procedure:**

1. Cut king-size sheet in half,  lengthwise or cut the fabric by the yard as described above.

2. Finish the sides with 1" hems. See Figure 5-10.

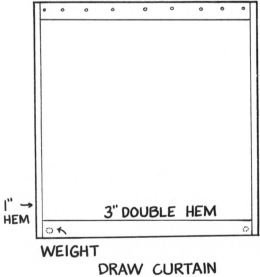

1"
HEM

3" DOUBLE HEM

WEIGHT

DRAW CURTAIN

**Figure 5-10**

3. Using the top hem already on your sheet or having made a 3" double hem on material by the yard, measure for placement of the 18 grommets or buttonholes which will hold the shower curtain rings. These holes are to be made 6" apart. Apply the grommets according to the manufacturer's instructions. Use your sewing machine at the buttonhole setting if you do not intend to use grommets. Buttonholes will do just as well.

4. Attach shower hooks to the holes.

5. Hang the hooks on the wires as shown in Figure 5-9.

6. Place rope through the shower hooks as pictured in Figure 5-9.

7. After your curtain has been hung in place, mark where the turn up for the hem should be with pins. Allow 6" so you can make a 3" double hem. Take down curtain.

8. After the hemming is completed, and before you close the sides, sew in the weights at the corners.

9. Spray with a fire retardant and rehang.

## MAKE CYLORAMAS IN A HURRY USING THESE SIX STEPS

See Figure 5-6.

**You Will Need:**

2 king size sheets or

18 yards of 60" wide material. Two widths will be needed for each section. Cut 6 pieces of material into 3-1/3 yards each.

Weights

Thumb tacks or heavy-duty staples

Fire retardant

**Procedure:**

1. Stitch two lengths together to make each section if material is by the yard, finish the sides of each section with 1" hems.

2. Make top hem, if your material is by the yard, allow 6" for a 3" double hem and stitch. If you are using a sheet, use the top hem without further stitching.

3. Measure for length with the help of the crew, who will hold the curtain in place. Mark with pins, allowing 6" for a 3" double hem.

4.  Before closing sides of the hem, sew in the weights at the corners.

5.  Use heavy staples or thumb tacks to fasten the cyclorama to the stage frame.

6.  Spray with flame retardant.

Now you have almost completed the project. However, those pulleys and curtain rings will show and they must be covered with an overhang. Here's how you can solve that problem and have a nice finished look to your stage setting.

## HOW TO MAKE AN OVERHANG

**You Will Need:** (See Figure 5-6)

9' aluminum clothesline wire

2 large nails

King-size sheet remnant or material by the yard

1.  Use the width of the king-size sheet (108") and cut a length of 7½". Turn under the top and bottom hems of 1¼" and stitch. See Figure 5-11.

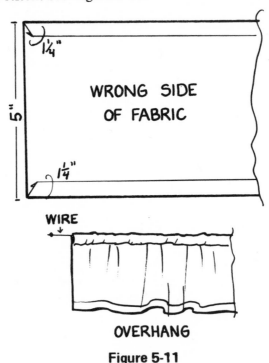

**Figure 5-11**

If you are using material by the yard, piece your 7½" lengths together until you get a width of 108". Turn under the hems and stitch.

2. String your wire through a hem and twist the ends around the nails which have been put in the posts. Make the wire as taut as possible.

Now your completed stage is ready for the actors to aquaint themselves with the setting, and the crew member in charge of drawing the curtains is ready to pull the rope and reveal the stage where action and entertainment will provide enjoyment for all.

Wherever you decide to give your play, find a staging area and use it creatively. Theater is an art, the product of adaptability and imagination (the "Let's Pretend" of children).

## BE FLEXIBLE HAVE FUN!

Keep in mind the following guidelines, and you *will* be flexible and you *will* have fun! Let's review:

1. Choose the stage setting that best suits the play and place where it will be given.

2. The use of a simple platform stage gives a psychological and practical lift to the actors and provides better visibility to the audience.

3. The building of the platforms and the making of the curtains by the students give the behind-the-scenes members a chance to show their work to the public.

4. Plan for the construction of the platforms as soon as possible so they can be used at rehearsals.

5. Plan for transportation of the portable stages if your presentation is to be given in a place other than your school.

Start the wheels of your scenery plans in motion at the same time as you are evaluating your staging. A plan of action for you to follow is in the next chapter.

CHAPTER **6**

# Time- and Work-Saving Formulas for Scenery Making

The houselights dim, the chattering and laughing stop. The audience's attention turns toward the parting curtains. Even though everyone knows from reading the program that the play takes place in the great hall of the king, everyone is wondering what the hall looks like behind those curtains.

The curtains part to reveal an impressive castle wall painted to look like stone, and upon this wall hang props of shields and colorful banners. Upstage center, a large "oaken" door with heavy-looking hinges and bolts is also part of the wall. The stage is set. The play has begun even before an actor has walked on stage.

Scenery is the physical background of the play, reinforcing significance and action, explaining place, period and mood, giving clues to the personality of the characters and their background. The scenery, props, costumes and lighting should combine to produce a harmonious effect.

## THE SECRET OF A SUCCESSFUL SET

One of simple design

One that is clearly seen and understood by the audience

One that is planned for easy construction

One that is planned for a minimum of painted details

Your principal colors will be determined by what type of play you are presenting. For example, a light comedy such as *The Importance of Being Ernest* would have a set with warm and cheerful colors, whereas a serious play like *Our Town* calls for a set with cool colors, as does a mystery. Plan colors that are bright and sparkling, offering exciting contrasts between dark and light when the play warrants it.

Choosing which type of set to make is, of course, largely due to the script's demands, the age and talents of the pupils and your budget. In addition, do you have the aid of the industrial arts department and art department? Can you involve parents and older pupils with manual skills to help with this exciting project?

## ZERO IN ON THE ONE-SET IDEA

Choosing a one-set play can solve those ever-present problems—not having enough time and its twin, not having a big enough budget. However, using a one-set play means you must not overburden the set with identical shapes and monotonous colors. Balance vertical lines with some horizontal ones. For instance, balance the vertical lines of the windows and doors with the horizontal lines of a couch or a long table. Hang a picture in an oval frame and drape back any curtains to further the use of curved lines for variety. Use some neutral color as well as your intense colors, since every painted detail is not of equal importance, paint the less important decoration in neutral colors. You need interest in a one-set arrangement, but it must not overwhelm and take the audience's attention away from the acting.

## FOUR TYPES OF SETS AND WHAT
## THEY HAVE TO OFFER

1. *Cyclorama (cyc):* See Chapter 5. This is a large curtain of neutral color fabric that hangs from a horizontal U-shaped metal or wooden frame suspended from the ceiling by pipes at the four corners. It is used for a background filler behind constructed scenery like a box set and also as a base for cut-out pieces, such as trees and doors which can be attached to the cyc with double faced tape. See Figures 6-1a and 6-1b.

2. *Drop:* This is a large sheet of plastic fabric or paper, usually framed, and hung from an overhead support. See Figure 6-2. It

HINGED SCREEN IN U-SHAPE WITH CUT-OUT ARCH
PLACED IN FRONT OF A CYCLORAMA

**Figure 6-1a**

CYCLORAMA AS A BASE FOR
CUT OUT DECORATIONS

**Figure 6-1b**

**Figure 6-2**

may be painted with poster paint on extra wide sheets of brown wrapping paper, or with acrylic paint on an inexpensive plastic dropcloth that is used by painters and comes in the size of 3 X 4 yds. (Available in most hardware and variety stores.) This type of background permits several quick, easy changes of scenery.

3. *Screen:* The three-paneled hinged screen is in itself a set or in the case of an improvised stage, can mask the entrances and exits of the actors. See Chapter 5. If no screens are available, you can make them of Masonite or plywood. Hinge these panels with loose pin hinges so the sections can be taken apart for easy moving and storing. Create any illusion you want—saw out the top areas into shapes such as treetops or rooftops, or for greater height, attach the cut out shapes to the tops of the screens. Even heavy cardboard cutouts taped on the screens will answer the purpose. Use your imagination. A screen set such as pictured in Figures 6-1a and 6-3 could easily be constructed by pupils in the industrial arts class.

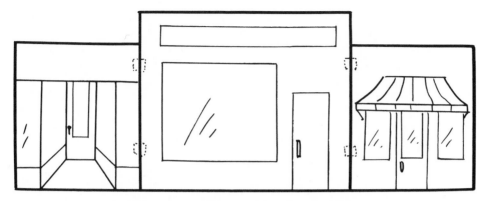

## HINGED  SCREEN  SHOWN  FLAT

**Figure 6-3**

4. *Flat Set (Flat)*: This is a fabric-covered wooden frame. The fabric (unbleached muslin is cheaper than canvas) is stapled and glued to the frame. Then it is sized with a coat of acrylic paint and decorated with any water-soluble paint. The making of the wooden frame requires more skill than the making of a screen and its construction should be done under the manual arts teacher's supervision. These frames can accommodate working doors and windows, so they must be squared up accurately. A simple set against a cyc background is a setting that you most likely will be using.

### A PLAN OF ACTION THAT SPEEDS YOU
### TOWARD YOUR SCENERY GOALS

It's a long way from seeing the set in your mind's eye to seeing it in its completed form. Here is a plan of action that can help you accomplish your scenery goals:

1. Draw what the set will look like, to scale if needed. Remember to bring into view all that the audience should see and block out all that the audience should not see, such as radiators, pipes and ropes.

2. Salvage any old sets that can be cleaned, mended and repainted.

3. Borrow from other schools.

4. Plan what has to be built.

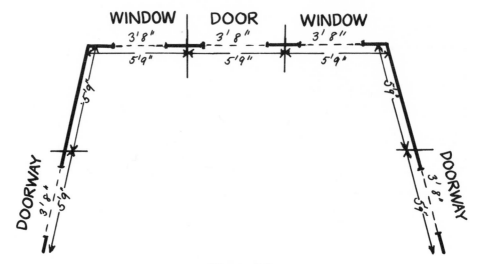

**Figure 6-4**

5. Draw a floor plan of the setting that not only includes doors, windows, fireplace and steps, but also shows where the separate units meet. See Figure 6-4.

6. Make a fairly detailed sketch of each unit of scenery, illustrating what you want painted on it.

7. When planning to use flats, draw a plan of each unit, showing dimensions and placement of door and window openings. See Figure 6-5.

8. Consult with the manual arts teacher, showing your plans and emphasizing the fact that the wood construction and the attaching of the muslin to the flats must be completed one week before the performance.

9. Consult with the art department teacher, showing the sketches, which include necessary details and color suggestions. If the scenery is to be copied exactly, either by the art department or the class, the sketch of the scene is first blocked in squares, then it can be enlarged on canvas. See Figure 6-6. Your timetable demands that the flats be completely painted by the thirteenth rehearsal, when crew and cast stage the pre-dress rehearsal. If your play is a video presentation, your scenery should be done in pastel colors, avoiding any glossy or reflective surfaces.

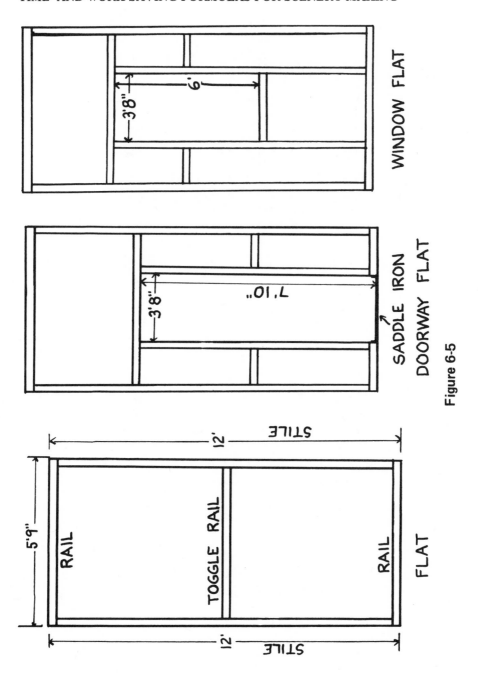

WINDOW FLAT

3'8"

6'

SADDLE IRON
DOORWAY FLAT

3'8"

7'10"

Figure 6-5

STILE

12'

5'9"

RAIL

TOGGLE RAIL

RAIL

STILE

12'

FLAT

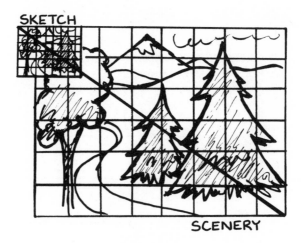

**Figure 6-6**

10. After the exact colors have been decided upon, tell your lighting supervisor what color gels will be needed for certain effects so he can order colors that need replacing. See Chapter 7.

11. Arrange for the transportation of scenery if it is created outside the school. If the Board of Education doesn't have a truck or minibus, enlist the help of a parent or business-man willing to use a station wagon or truck to transport the scenery. And remember your custodian is your best ally in setting up and striking the set.

Here are the construction plans to further help you accomplish your scenery goals. These tell how to construct screens and flats.

### YOUR EASY-TO-FOLLOW PLAN FOR CONSTRUCTING SCREENS

See Figures 6-1a and 6-3.

Screens can be made of Masonite or plywood. Both surfaces take paint easily. Use loose pin hinges (see Figure 6-7) so the sections can be taken apart for easy moving and storage. When ordering your lumber, give the lumber person your measured foot, and let him do the converting. Masonite and plywood are available in the following sizes: Masonite . . .1/4" thick . . .4' X 8' . . .4' X 10"

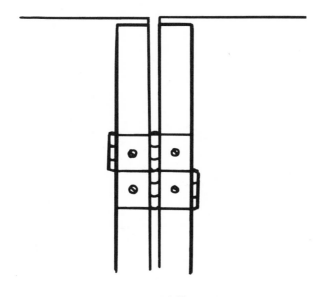

**Figure 6-7**

. . .4' X 12" sheets; they also can be cut to order at the lumber yard. Plywood . . .1/4" thick . . .4' X 8' sheets or cut to order.

### You Will Also Need:

Furring strips. . . 1 1/2" X 2 1/2" for back brace and base for hinges

Loose pin hinges. . . two for each hinged section

Countersink screws

Bolts

Plastic wood

Acrylic paint for prime coat

White glue

Water-base paint for design

### Procedure:

See Figure 6-8.

Use flathead screws to mount furring strips along the edges of the back of the panels to be joined. The holes should be countersunk when the screws are tightened to hold the furring strip. Fill the holes with caulking compound or glazier's putty.

Mount the hinges on the back of the mounted furrings strips so that the panels can be closed for storage or positioning.

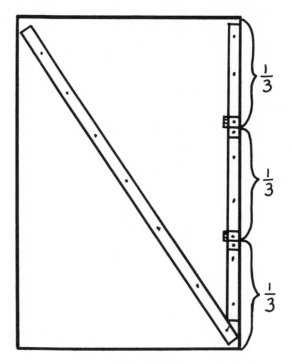

$\frac{1}{3}$

$\frac{1}{3}$

$\frac{1}{3}$

**Figure 6-8**

To join more than two panels, use hinges, but remove the pins when they are to be folded or stored.

To brace the panel, use wood screws to mount a furring strip diagonally across each panel.

## DISCOVER HOW TO MAKE FLAT SCENERY (FLATS)

**You Will Need:**

Wood (Pine) 2" X 2"

Loose pin hinges or lash cleats. . . or 16 penny spikes. . .or 2" blue screws

Angle irons for open doorways and arches

Unbleached muslin

Sash cord, if using lashline instead of hinges

Corner braces

#8 carpet tacks or industrial stapler

Acrylic or other water-based paint

Flat right-angle plates

T plates

Nails

Plastic wood

White glue

## Procedure:

1. Place top and bottom rails on floor.

2. Place side stiles between them.

3. Place center rails so they divide the flat into two equal parts. See Figure 6-5.

4. Check angles with metal right angle.

5. Cross nail at right angles, after checking corners for true right angles.

6. Wood glue ALL joints in addition to using nails and screws.

7. Install right-angle mending plates and T plates, nails and screws.

8. Make plywood corners and keystones.

   a. Cut corners in triangles 8" X 8".

   b. Cut keystones 6" X 3". (Sizes can vary to need.)

9. For maximum reinforcement, install corners and keystones 3/4" from top and sides. Use clout nails set in the thickness of the lumber, so the flat can be set at an angle to each other and fit together. See Figure 6-9.

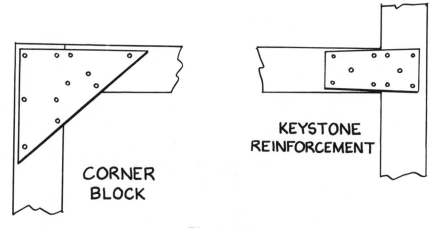

CORNER
BLOCK

KEYSTONE
REINFORCEMENT

**Figure 6-9**

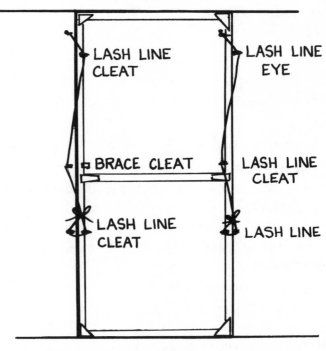

LASHLINE  HARDWARE  PLACEMENT

**Figure 6-10**

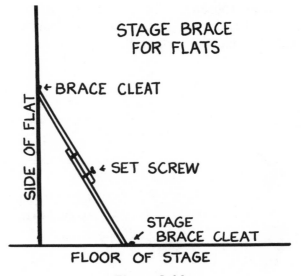

**Figure 6-11**

10. If you are using hinges instead of lashlines, follow hinge directions under "screens."

11. Install the lashline cleats, using cleats just for that, or 16 penny nails or 2" blue screws. See Figure 6-10.

  a. First cleat is 18" from top of left-hand corner.

  b. Second cleat is 1' above the center on the right side of the flat.

  c. Third cleat is 1' below the center on the left side of the flat.

  d. Fourth and fifth cleats are directly opposite each other on either side of the flat, 3' from the bottom.

  e. After the flat is completed and ready to be set up, attach lashline as shown in Figure 6-10.

  f. Follow Figure 6-11 for brace for flats.

12. Measure for the muslin.

  Allow about 2" of the fabric to extend around the perimeter of the frame for fastening purposes.

  Fabric that is 72" wide is right for the frame which is usually 69" wide (5'9").

13. After the muslin is cut in the correct lengths and the selvage removed, it is attached to the frames in the following manner:

  a. Lay the frame on the floor, smooth side up so the side with the corner reinforcements is next to the floor.

  b. Lay the muslin across the frame. Do not stretch or pull the fabric.

  c. Fasten each corner with a #8 carpet tack driven only part way into the wood. The muslin should be taut but not stretched out of shape.

  d. Tack the muslin all the way around in the following manner:

  First, tack muslin across the top. Tack 1/2" from the inner edge of the frame. This applies to all tacking. Place the tacks 6" apart. Now tack the sides and other end (Figure 6-12). Remove temporary tacks at corners.

  e. Turn under the loose fabric and glue it to the frame. Use glue sparingly.

  f. To make the fabric really taut, spray with water from a

**Figure 6-12**

garden hose with the nozzle turned to the finest spray and let dry naturally.

g. Prime with acrylic, using it flowingly, but not too wet. This is to fill in the minute holes in the fabric.

h. Dry naturally and paint your design.

*Special support for flats:* See Figure 6-11. Brace is 1" X 1" wood held together with clamps. One end has a forked hook to fit stage brace cleat, the other end has an iron heel which fits into the brace cleat on the flat. This cleat is attached on the flat 8' or more from the flat.

When an arch is required for the main entrance, you can use these plans. Remember when you have an arch, you will need some scenery in back of it, called a *"mask."*

## HOW TO CONSTRUCT A DOOR ARCH

See Figure 6-13.

**Figure 6-13**

**Procedure:**

    1. Make paper pattern.

Draw 1/2 of arch to size.

Draw a second line 3" away from the first, following the shape of the first line.

Fold and cut out, making a complete arch.

Place on wood, trace outline for cutting.

    2. When constructing a flat for an archway, omit the crossrail which forms the top of doors.

Connect lower ends of arch to top sides of door frame.

A rail is placed at the top of the arch.

Two short rails are nailed between the arch opening and the sides of the flat with keystones.

The top rail is attached with keystones to the sides and a triangle to the arch.

Fasten muslin and paint.

When your class constructs the scenery, you will be faced with space problems and the hall may have to be the working and storage area. Time may require that some of the work be done during lunch hour. Painting time can be cut down by using stencils for similarly shaped subjects. Instruct your scenery painters to work in large masses and to avoid small details that will be lost on stage. The scenery making can be a very important art project for the year, giving a valuable lesson in composition, color and technique, and an opportunity for the. pupils to work as a group; furthermore, their work will be seen and appreciated by the class, the school and the community.

## DOORWAYS TO INNOVATIVE SCENERY MAKING

How about using scenery in more creative ways? Would you like the opportunity to have as many children as possible seen on stage? These budget-saving and production-expanding ideas can come to your aid if yours is an elementary grade presentation.

Tape large sheets of paper, either painted or decorated with cutouts, to:

Portable bulletin boards

Moveable blackboards

Clothes trees

Nurse's room screens

Large packing cases

Clothes line or wire

OR

Present decorated sheets of paper by having:

Some of the children stand in place holding the paper.

Two pupils slowly unroll the scenery as the story line of the play progresses.

A group carry and hold in place, thick cardboard cutouts of houses, doors, etc., with another group forming a curtain in front of them, keeping the scenery from view until it is in place.

A group standing on different steps of stepladders with the scenic cutouts.

**Let's Review:**

1. Plan carefully for the scenery, making it clear to others what you expect.

2. Check to see if the construction and decorating are progressing on schedule.

3. In an elementary school production, rely on your custodian for help in the setting up and the striking (taking down) of the set.

4. If the scenery can be used again, see that it is safely stored away.

5. Don't forget scenery painters should get recognition in the program.

Light your scenery and actors in the best possible ways. Use the guidelines in the next chapter.

# CHAPTER 7

# Lighting...Your Switched-On Magic

Gil Wechsler, lighting designer of the Metropolitan Opera House, New York, said in *The New York Times.* "The basic idea is that the performing arts are co-operative enterprises. A single person's contribution should not make or break a show. " Your lighting crew will be a valuable part of the production as is the crew at the "Met." That crew may have 300 lights to attend to during an average performance, and be 30 members strong, but your crew will be just as important. Mr. Wechsler considers them as important as the stars. Be sure your people take a bow.

You, of course, won't have a monumental number of lights and controls to illuminate the play. The production most likely will require some lighting, so preparation will have to be done early so that the lighting rehearsal will go smoothly.

## HOW LIGHTING CUES ARE WRITTEN AND READ

In your director's book the cues for the various lighting situations will be added—colors, dimming, fading, etc. The cues will read like this:

Cue #1—House light down.

Cue #2—Special spots on balcony front-amber filters, up; and so on throughout the play.

Cue sheets will be made and given to the members of the lighting staff.

## HOW TO USE COLOR FILTERS SUCCESSFULLY

The filters (gels) are your source of colored light. These sheets of colored plastic fit in front of the lamp (bulb), and the lamp's beam of light will project the color. The filters are affected by the intense heat of the lamps, so when purchasing new filters try to get acetate or vinyl filters. Those made of polyesters or polycarbonates have the highest melt temperatures. The dyes on or in the filters can also be affected by the intense heat as well as the plastic itself. The entire filter can fall victim to the tungsten halogen lamp which has become the standard source of stage lighting. Avoid using dark greens because they will become heat damaged faster than reds regardless of their particular plastic base.

Your crew will be checking to see if the colored filters are in good condition. They may have to order new ones for replacement or special ones for this production. A scratch on a filter is all right on an unfocused light, but is evident on a focused spot.

For best results in dealing with the heat problem, follow these suggestions:

The filter should be held securely all around the frame perimeter. Fasten the filter down with double-face polyester tape, or use brass paper fasteners to keep it in place in at least four points of contact.

If you see a sagging filter, replace it because the filter is melting and it will produce a distorted light.

Costumes, scenery, season, mood and time of day give you the basis for the colors of light to be used. Early knowledge of costume and scenery colors is essential for the color cues in the director's book as mentioned.

Send for the filter color samples from the following manufacturers: For samples of colored filters, write:

Rosco Laboratories, Inc.
36 Bush Avenue
Port Chester, New York 10573

For a catalog of color listings of filters, write:

Edmund Scientific Company
1776 Edscorp Building
Barrington, New Jersey 08007

It is good to keep up to date with the latest filter colors because there are always changes. It is advisable to get a new sample book every three years, and if the manufacturer doesn't have it dated, you should make a notation.

## COLOR TESTING CAN BE A SNAP

Not only can you use the acetate samples when choosing color filters, but you can make slides from them. Take the samples, cut them to size, fit them into cardboard slide frames, and show them by using a Kodak Carousel. This way you can test the filter colors on the fabrics, scenery and actors' complexions. If your play is staged in a small area, this method of lighting could be used. They can have designs painted on them—see Chapter 10, "Special Effects."

Colors, as you probably know, fall into two families: warm or cold.

$$
\begin{array}{ll}
\text{WARM} & \left\{ \begin{array}{l} \text{straw (beiges)} \\ \text{pinks} \\ \text{ambers} \\ \text{blues} \end{array} \right. \\
\text{COLD} & \left\{ \begin{array}{l} \text{greens} \\ \text{grays} \end{array} \right.
\end{array}
$$

## SIMPLE GUIDELINES FOR COLOR
## LIGHT PLANNING

1. Avoid using the opposite color when lighting costumes or scenery—a red beam on a green dress will make it look gray. See Figure 7-1 for color guide.

2. Choose a color of similar hue to that which is to be illuminated. This will enhance the color of the fabric and make it more prominent.

3. When using an amber filter, have the actors apply more rouge than usual to avoid sallow-looking complexions.

4. If a red filter has to be used, have the actors use a rouge with a bluish tone, otherwise the red light will be reflected and the rouge will not show.

5. If a blue filter is used, you will be faced with a different

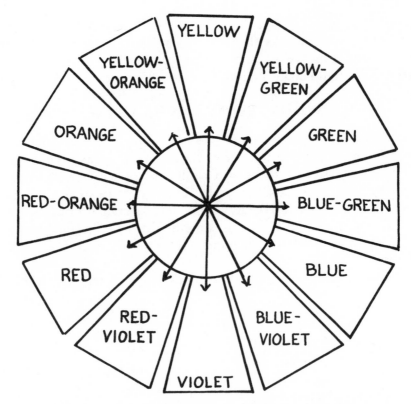

## COLOR GUIDE SHOWING COLOR OPPOSITES

**Figure 7-1**

problem. The rouge will appear as two black spots. Use a light foundation with just a trace of rouge.

6. Avoid using green since it gives an unearthly appearance. It would, however, do great things for Dracula.

7. Take heart, the pinks and light lavenders will enhance the complexions of all the actors.

This list has dealt with lighting the actors per se, however, there is the overall "look" to the lighting that must be considered. Visibility, composition and mood are all part of the play. The basic function of lighting is visibility. The audience must hear and see. The lighting can be controlled, so details can be emphasized or a whole area can be obscured. This leads to the importance of composition which is revealed through both the creative and practical use of light and shadow. Light has space-filling properties which can aid the actor with his movement within that space. It can also extend the believability of the scenery; for example, if your script calls for a lighted fireplace on a side wall, you need the look of a warm glow on the surrounding furniture and on the actors. Two small amber and red spotlights placed low and concealed from view will provide this touch of realism.

Mood or atmosphere is the total visual effect. Use warm tones for a comedy or a light drama, and use the cool tones for a mystery, a tragedy or a play dealing with the abstract. The use of correct color puts the audience in a sympathetic mood with the play.

## HOW YOUR LIGHTING SYSTEM WORKS

When theatre moved from the outdoors to the indoors, crude lighting was devised. However, dramatists began to demand better and better lighting. They knew it could be controlled and improved upon. Today we have computerized controls with memory systems. Your setup probably is a control box of simple switches which is located to the right of the proscenium stage and connected to these switches are your lights which are probably some of the following types:

### Floodlights

These lights provide a wide-angle beam spread. The unit pictured is a fixed spread floodlight, other units can be focused. See Figure 7-2.

**Figure 7-2**

Figure 7-3A

Figure 7-3B

**Spotlights**

"Fresnelites" Special lights from Strand Century, a theatrical lighting company. Fresnel is pronounced Fra-nel. (See Figures 7-3A and 7-3B.) The units pictures are Tunsten Halogen (quartz) lamps and have the following features:

1. High intensity.
2. Narrow spot to wide flood with soft edge.
3. Externally operated focusing.
4. Hinged die-cast front door with integral frame for color filters and barn door sides.

"Lekolite" also from the same company. These can use either the long life Tunsten Halogen lamps or the conventional incandescent ones. See Figure 7-4.

The unit has the following features:

1. Compact design 4 1/2" X 6".
2. Ellipsoidal reflector for maximum light gathering and evenness of field.
3. Spring loaded latches for easy maintenance.
4. Secure and accurate positioning by means of the die cast aluminum yoke.

**Figure 7-4**

**Borderlights**

These units are portable, efficient and versatile. These strong features make for successful toning and blending of the acting area and the cyclorama. See Figure 7-5.

1.  They have a large choice of colored lamps to be used in the unit.
2.  A spring hinged door provides easy access for relamping and servicing.
3.  Available in three-or four-color circuits.
4.  Heat resisting, glass diffusing roundels are included with all units.
5.  These units can be mounted to pipes, ceilings or floors and come equipped with pigtails for interconnections.

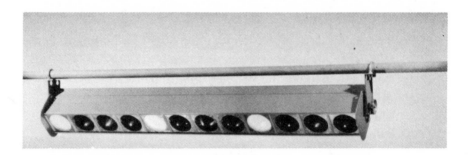

**Figure 7-5**

**Control System**

Pictured in Figure 7-6, is the Micro-Q modularly designed two-scene manual preset system from Strand Century. The school fortunate enough to have a unit such as this is providing the lighting director with a system which has the following features:

1.  Optional plug-in memory module.
2.  10 submaster module available.
3.  Dipless split cross-fader.
4.  Independent preset switch for each controller.
5.  Independent master.
6.  Grand master.

7.  Future expansion in groups of eight controllers.

8.  Non-dim controls.

9.  Houselight and panic controls.

Compact portable lighting systems are also available. For a catalog of lighting equipment and systems, write:

Strand Century, Inc.
20 Bushes Lane
Elmwood Park, New Jersey 07407

**Figure 7-6**

## EFFECTIVE CONTROLLING OF INTENSITY,
## FORM AND MOVEMENT

To be most effective, lighting equipment should supply the desired output of light in intensity, form, color and movement thus producing the dramatic effect you wish to convey.

### Intensity

It can be controlled by the use of particular lights, mounting positions, choice of filter colors and use of dimmers.

The intensity of the light on the stage is in direct relation to the distance of the light source from the stage and to the wattage of the lamp used.

Avoid too little light or a rapid succession of intensity variations because these situations tend to confuse and tire the audience.

### Form

A particular quality of light beam is given by each piece of equipment described in this chapter. These instruments can give a hard-or soft-edge beam, a narrow or wide spread angle, a smooth or mottled effect.

Determine the placement of your equipment by the directions you want the beams to take.

Appropriate angles give the height and impressiveness you desire.

Position your light source according to the shadow you want to show—long shadows at early morning and afternoon. Different shadows at night.

### Color

This is used to accent, enhance and even distort the scene. The color filters, as mentioned before, are placed in front of each lamp. These filtered light beams, used in conjunction with dimmers, will provide your needs.

If you change from a warm tone to a cool one, you must first fade down the warm one and fade up the cool one.

Striplights, your blending and toning unit, should include amber and white filters to obtain tints with brightness.

### Movement

It means there is a change in one or all of the qualities of light.

It must be carefully handled during the play, changing on cue, to a rhythm, tempo or timing that relates directly to the action.

It will elevate all visual aspects of the play.

## PLUNGE INTO LIGHTING FOR MOOD OR ATMOSPHERE

There are certain general methods that can serve as guides for any type of production on any type of stage, but the application of these guides will vary for each production.

### Acting Area Lights

These lights comprise a special group of units that illuminate each playing space separately from the rest of the stage. Downstage portions of the stage, in front of the proscenium, are usually lighted with Lekolite spotlights. Upstage areas are illuminated with Fresnelites and Lekolites are placed behind the proscenium.

### Toning and Blending Lights

These lights give atmosphere over the acting area and stage with color tones. Borderlights and floodlights, placed above the acting area, will give virtually shadowless illumination and will accommodate a large range of color.

### Background Lighting

This term is usually used when dealing with light on scenery that appears in a proscenium type of stage.

Cyclorama overhead floods or striplights and cyclorama foots are frequently used as are backing and ground row striplights.

### Backlights

These light sources provide lighting on the actor's head and shoulders, creating a halo effect that separates the player from the background.

### Followspots

These spots illuminate the actor regardless of whatever type of other lighting is being used, and their beams will travel with the actor's movements on stage.

### Special Lights

These lights either emphasize objects, such as doors or furniture, or they convey the illusion of sunlight or moonlight.

These spots with the addition of templates, can produce a city skyline, clouds, trees, abstract patterns, etc. Further information concerning this type of lighting procedure is found in Chapter 10, "Special Effects."

Even though "The play's the thing," the physical facilities must be evaluated. Just how adequate is your lighting system? Remember, seeing the action is very important. Turn on those lights with your crew and the custodian, and they will clue you in to what is working well and what isn't.

## PROSCENIUM STAGE LIGHTING TECHNIQUES
## THAT REALLY WORK

Proscenium stage lighting should have the following equipment:

6 Fresnel spotlights

These will provide soft edged flood lighting and color blending for the general acting area.

6 500 watt Fresnel spot medium prefocus lamps

6 color filters

Check to see if the colors already in use are the ones you want to use.

A dimmer board

Lighting packages, which include the necessary lights and a portable dimmer, may be purchased from:

> Times Square Theatrical and Studio Supply Corp.
> 318 West 47 Street
> New York, NY 10036

A more fully equipped lighting system covering an entire stage with blending color lights will include:

8 Fresnel spotlights

These do the work as mentioned above, and provide unobstructed overlapping of light. This number of lights can give a floodlighting and color blending combination over a wide area.

8 500-watt lamps for the Fresnels

9 ellipsoidal spotlights

These are usually used for illuminating the forward acting areas, highlighting, and projecting patterns.

9 500-watt lamps for ellipsoidal lights

3 scoop floodlights

These are good for lighting backdrops and to fill in the acting area.

3 500-watt lamps for the scooplights

20 color filters

1 dimmer board

Color frames are separate from the lights, so be sure you have enough for your needs.


## WHY LIGHTING THE ARENA STAGE IS DIFFERENT

When your play is presented on an arena or three-quarter (thrust) stage, your lighting will be of a different order. A fully equipped theatre of this type will have overhead lighting. However, if you have to improvise with this kind of layout, you will be using standing lights. These of course, will have to be kept out of the audience's eyes.

When lighting an arena or thrust stage, this type of lighting system is used:

4 spotlights with Fresnel lenses and adjustable beam.

Colored filters not necessary.

Place them approximately 20' - 25' feet from the audience.

Focus the lights on the actors; do not light the surrounding audience.

Provide adequate space in gallery front for the placement of the mounted lights and for the lighting operator, if he is using a portable lighting board.

Pay attention to where the electrical cables are placed, so there is easy movement around them.

If your presentation makes unusual demands on the lighting crew or is to be outdoors, consider using a professional lighting service.

## FUN WAYS OF GETTING MAXIMUM RESULTS
## WITH MINIMUM LIGHTING AND COST

Perhaps at this point in the chapter you are saying, "The information given so far is fine for those who are putting on a play in well-equipped surroundings with lots of help from older students. I'm putting on a play with third graders, the staging will have to be improvised, as well as the lighting and I have a shoe-string budget. What suggestions do you have for me?"

You can refer to Chapter 5 for directions for making a portable stage, if an elevation is needed. Following are some suggestions for simple lighting:

Large size flashlights make good spotlights for the illumination of small areas.

Bridge lamps can be used for side lighting.

Floor or table lamps work when foil reflectors are made for them.

1-quart metal juice cans wired for electricity are very effective. See the following instructions:

## BUILD YOUR OWN ALL-PURPOSE LIGHT

See the following instructions:

This easy-to-make light can be used as part of a footlight system, or it can serve as a small spotlight. It's simple to mount for either use, and when tied in with a switchboard, a group of them can be used to provide some of the special lighting effects that can make a ho-hum play come alive.

All you need is a large juice can, a 50 watt reflector bulb, a ceiling mounting fixture and a length of line cord with a plug.

For footlight use and limited spot applications, the 50 watt bulb will be more than adequate. There are larger bulbs available and you can get larger cans to make brighter units, but for most school plays this unit should do the trick. The bulb has a built-in reflector which concentrates the light. Therefore, even though the bulb is rated at only 50 watts, it is more effective than a conventional globe-type 50 watt bulb. If you don't believe this, test one against the other.

The juice can serves only to protect the bulb; it doesn't contain any reflector system. Even though the light is directed out in one direction and most of the heat will be dissipated near the

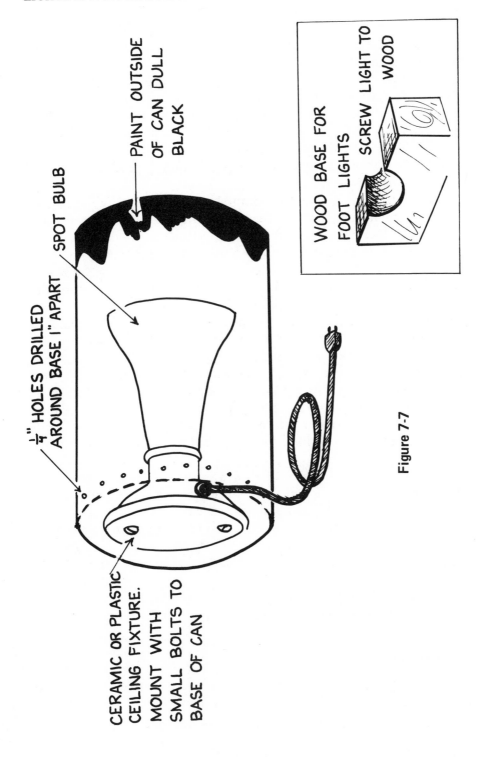

PAINT OUTSIDE OF CAN DULL BLACK

SPOT BULB

$\frac{1}{4}$" HOLES DRILLED AROUND BASE 1" APART

CERAMIC OR PLASTIC CEILING FIXTURE. MOUNT WITH SMALL BOLTS TO BASE OF CAN

WOOD BASE FOR FOOT LIGHTS

SCREW LIGHT TO WOOD

Figure 7-7

opening, it is still a good idea to drill a number of 1/4" holes around the base of the can. This will provide for a convection flow of air to cool and extend the life of the bulb.

The ceramic or plastic mounting base can be bought at just about any hardware or electrical supply house. Some are made with switches and some without. You probably will be controlling the light from a remote location, so the switch in the base may not be needed. If you do not need the switch, but cannot get a unit without one, you can use the switchable unit, but leave it in the "on" position all the time.

The ceiling fixture is mounted to the base of the juice can with two small bolts. Just center the fixture and use it as a template to mark the location of the holes.

There is one place to watch very carefully when you make this lamp, and that is the hole through which the line cord will pass. No matter how carefully you file and finish the edge of the hole, it will still be sharp enough to cut through the insulation if the wire is tugged often enough or pulled sharply. You can install a conventional rubber grommet in the hole—made for this purpose—or you can simply take a few turns of tape around the wire where it passes through the can. *Be sure to protect the wire—and the players!*

Normally, we would suggest that you paint the outside of the can a dull black. But, if the light is to blend in with other colors in use on the stage, paint the can accordingly. In fact, you can paint the can as often as you like, to blend with the colors of other plays you do.

*A word of caution:* If you are using this, or other lamps as footlights, be very careful to place the cords well out of the paths of the actors who are treading on the boards.

Floodlights can be constructed out of wooden boxes. Line the boxes with aluminum foil, bore holes for electrical wiring, and screw base-socket receptacles in the boxes and attach extension cords to them.

There is nothing quite like being on stage in the spotlight. The moment those lights go on, your pupils will be turned on and tuned in to acting.

### Let's Review:

1.  Add lighting cues to director's book. And give cue sheets to lighting crew.
2.  Check filters for condition—order new ones.

3.  Experiment with lights before the actual light rehearsal.

4.  Consider renting or using a professional service if your presentation is highly unusual or out of doors.

Behind the curtain, the stage lights are lit, out front the house lights are dimming, everyone on either side is ready—the play is about to begin!

Further lighting information on special effects is in Chapter 10.

Strand Century was most helpful in providing information and photographs for this chapter.

# CHAPTER 8

# Easy, Enjoyable Ways to
# Costume the Play

Now is the time to dress up the actors.

Acting is a game of let's pretend that the children have been playing since the age of three. All of us have encountered the home-grown cowboys, supermen, astronauts, doctors, nurses, monsters and "grown ups" in costumes of their own creation. How often a bath towel is Batman's cape.

The play you are presenting, however, requires careful planning of the costumes to carry a definite message to the audience. At a glance, the audience should recognize the types of characters that are involved and just anything will not do!

Anything worn by an actor is a costume. It may be contemporary clothing specified in the play; it may be parts of conventional wearing apparel, such as boots or a muffler. Or, the costume may be an elaborately trimmed garment, such as a king's robe. A costume is always needed, not only to explain the part in the play, but to heighten interest.

## HOW TO WORK EFFECTIVELY WITH
## DETAILS AND COLOR

A period play requires some research. Dresses and suits should be in keeping with the period. Some details are needed, but they should not be lost up on the stage. Notice in the photo, Figure 8-1, there are no unnecessary details on the costumes.

**Figure 8-1**

However, if your production is in a theatre-in-the-round setting, careful attention to detail is essential in terms of design as well as sewing. The audience is extremely close to the actors, so that a pinned hem or an out-of-period accessory will be certainly noticed.

Because most school stages are at eye level, attention should be given to the footwear. For example, Prince Charming in gym shoes spoils the effect. Nevertheless, these same gym shoes may be worn by Prince Charming, if covered with felt to look like those shoes worn by a prince. Bedroom slippers are easily adapted to look like period footwear.

The costume coordinator should be aware of the fact that crowns, swords, trailing gowns and the like may cause problems at performance time. Parts of the costume or substitutions should be used as early as the third rehearsal. What a disaster it would be if King Arthur's crown wiggled, Queen Guinevere became tangled in her gown or Columbus tripped on his sword! Such comic effects are desired only if the play requires it.

The costume coordinator should be responsible for the color combinations of the costumes, scenery and props. When the purple gown is settled on the *very* orange sofa, the effect is definitely unsettling.

Avoid repeating costume colors on the characters that appear on stage at the same time, and dress the sympathetic characters in warm hues from the red or yellow families. These are advancing colors and they make objects appear nearer and bigger. A colored spotlight, the same hue as the costume, emphasizes the costume color.

Comic characters may wear outlandish or exaggerated costumes in clashing colors to heighten the humor of their roles. For example, the effect of Cinderella's step-sisters' purple and scarlet gowns against that *very* orange sofa would add to the fun.

If your play is a video presentation; plan to have costumes of pastel or soft medium colors. Avoid white as well as checkered or striped prints.

## THE SIX-POINT PLAN FOR THE
## COSTUME COORDINATOR

**Step One** . . .With a list of the actors and their costumes, the costume coordinator should check with the cast and make a record of the costume parts they can supply themselves. When these come in, each should be tagged with the owner's name so everything can be returned promptly after the performance. If headdresses and masks are part of any costume, the planning of them begins now. Because most of them are made from paper and papier-mâché, see Chapter 9 for step-by-step techniques for using the materials.

**Step Two** . . .The coordinator, should salvage what can be collected from the school costume closet, and embark on the next step. Gather ready-made garments and accessories that the students can supply and purchase what is available at thrift shops, flea markets, antique and rummage sales. Often ready-mades can be adapted easily to costume specifications.

Although wigs are not often required, fairly inexpensive acrylic models are available at department and variety stores.

**Step Three** . . .Evaluate the costumes and accessories gathered through the sources mentioned, and consider a rental agency for the missing material. Renting is best when actors are to be dressed in elaborate costumes; there is no substitute for the professional powdered wig. That impressive looking tux that's needed just might not exist in anyone's closet, nor is it certain that the available suit will fit. A rental agency will solve that problem. Refer to the Yellow Pages for formal wear and costume renters. However, because rentals cost money, the actor won't be wearing the tux until the performance. From the third rehearsal on, he should be using a jacket to acquire a casual ease in wearing it. The costume coordinator should also supply a substitution for that rented mink stole or fancy jewelry.

**Step Four** . . .At this point, the costume coordinator faces the most important aspect of the job; she must make some of the costumes and accessories herself. She can choose to use some of the patterns in this chapter or buy ready-made patterns. She should measure the cast and calculate the amount of fabric needed and plan the use of trimmings, decorations, zippers and other findings.

**Step Five** . . .The costume coordinator must consult the director's book at this point for the names and telephone numbers of parents and other volunteers willing to work on the costumes. (See Chapter 3.)

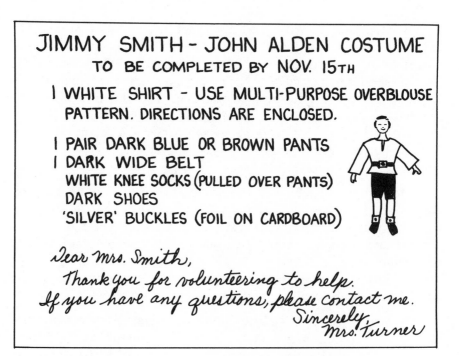

**Figure 8-2**

**Step Six** . . .Each of the sewing volunteers receives a pack which includes patterns and sewing instructions. If possible, fabric should be included. A friendly note should be sent with the pack which includes a list of costume requirements and a simple sketch of the costume. See Figure 8-2. The costume coordinator then checks the fit of the costume at the pre-dress rehearsal, when all the customes are ready. From then on, there must be a secure place to store the costumes and wigs, which can be lightly covered with plastic to maintain their fresh appearance.

## ANYONE CAN SEW COSTUMES USING THESE PATTERNS

Most of the popular costumes for school plays can be made from the following patterns. Sizes can be altered easily, and simple embellishments can change a colonial farmer's blouse into a king's tunic. The skills needed can often be found in the Home Economics class, with willing parents or with your own class.

PATTERN                        COSTUME SUGGESTIONS

Multi-purpose coverall                clown
See Figure 8-3.                       astronaut
                                      wizard
                                      animal

**Figure 8-3**

Multi-purpose overblouse
(short version)

**SHORT OVERBLOUSE**

**Figure 8-4**

king
nobleman
peasant
frontiersman
Asian farmer
mandarin
Pilgrim
Colonial artisan
Colonial farmer
Central and South
  American farmer-worker
American Indian
Asian Indian
African man's dashiki
Eskimo's parka

**Figure 8-5**

**LONG OVERBLOUSE**

Multi-purpose overblouse
(long version)

ghost
witch
Japanese lady's kimono
desert dweller
flapper

Basic long dress
See Figure 8-6.

medieval lady
Pilgrim
colonist
European peasant's
    holiday dress

1800's - 1900

DUTCH

Figure 8-6

SPANISH

COLONIAL          PILGRIM

MEDIEVAL          PIONEER

**Figure 8-6** (continued)

Notice in Figure 8-6, how the look of the basic dress is changed through the use of different accessories, neck lines and skirt lengths. It can be adapted to any time in history from the Middle Ages until the end of the 19th century and it can become the dress of various nationalities.

There are patterns for popular costume accessories in this book. They are the bolero and vest, Pilgrim collar, Pilgrim and Dutch cap, pioneer bonnet, cap, mobcap, cape, apron and bustle.

Instructions for making a tabard are included in this chapter. The tabard is a quick and easy costuming idea, which lends itself to a variety of situations. Leotards complete the costume. See Figure 8-7.

TABARD IDEAS

**Figure 8-7**

## DISCOVER HOW TO MAKE PATTERNS

Measure the actor to determine which size pattern is needed. Consult the size chart, Figure 8-8 and How to Measure illustration in Figure 8-9. If the pattern illustration doesn't show a large enough size, add 1/2" for each larger size needed, or subtract 1/2" for each smaller size.

| MEASUREMENT CHART FOR SIZES | | | | | |
|---|---|---|---|---|---|
| | 4-6 | 7-8 | 10-12 | 14 FEMALE | 14 MALE |
| CHEST | 23"-25" | 26"-27" | 28"-30" | 32" | 32" |
| WAIST | 21"-22" | 23"-24" | 25"-26" | 26½" | 27" |
| HIP | 24"-26" | 27"-28" | 29"-31" | 34" | 32½" |
| BACK | 9½"-10" | 11"-12" | 12¾"-13½" | 14½" | 15" |

**Figure 8-8**

To convert the grid patterns to actual size:

**You Will Need:**

Right Triangle
Ruler
Pencil
Pen
Large piece of paper, such as wrapping paper

Use the right triangle and ruler to measure the squares. Each square equals 2".

Copy the pattern as illustrated, in pencil. Progress one square at a time. Check and retrace the penciled outline with a pen. Be sure to mark the arrows which indicate the straight of the fabric. Also mark boldly where the pattern is to be placed on the fold of the fabric and where special stitching occurs. The seam allowance is 5/8" unless stated otherwise.

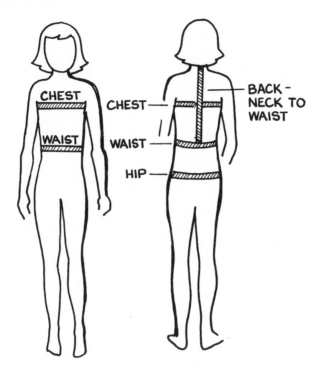

**Figure 8-9**

Cut out the pattern.

Be sure each piece is clearly marked as to size and part.

*How to sew the following garments:* a Multi-Purpose Cover-all, an Overblouse, a Basic Long Dress, a Bolero or Vest, a Pilgrim Cap and Collar, a Pioneer Bonnet, a Cap, a Colonial Mobcap, a Cape, an Apron, and a Bustle.

### THE MULTI-PURPOSE COVERALL

See Figures 8-3, 8-10 and 8-11.

The amount of fabric needed is indicated below:

| Sizes 4 – 6 | 7 – 8 | 10 – 12 |
|---|---|---|
| 2 7/8 yds. 36" wide | 3 3/8 yds. 36" wide | 4 1/8 yds. 36" wide |
| 2 1/4 yds. 45" wide | 2 3/8 yds. 45" wide | 3 yds. 45" wide |

**You Will Need:**

One neckline zipper, or

Bias tape for tie at neck opening

Before making the pattern, measure for individual sleeve and leg lengths. Allow for 2" hems.

**Procedure:**

Enlarge the grid pattern to scale as indicated in Figures 8-10 and 8-11.

Copy the pattern.

Cut out the pattern parts.

Fold the fabric so it is double and the selvages match.

Lay the pattern parts on the fabric and pin them in place. Cut out the fabric.

Stitch the front center seam from the crotch to the neck. Reinforce the seam with a second stitching.

Trim the seam 1/4" from the stitching.

Press the seam open.

Apply glitter, appliques, paint, etc.

Stitch the back center seam from the crotch to the dot indicated on the pattern in Figure 8-11.

Reinforce the seam with a second stitching.

Trim the seam 1/4" from the stitching.

Press the seam open.

Stitch the zipper to the garment, following the zipper manu-facturer's instructions or stitch down a 5/8" seam allowance on either side of the back opening if you are using a bias tape tie for a neck closing.

Pin the front and the back of the garment together with right sides facing each other.

Stitch the sleeve seams from wrist to neck.

Press the seams open.

Stitch the outer seam of the garment by starting at the bottom of the legs and continuing to the end of the sleeves.

Stitch the inner leg seams.

Press the seams open.

Try the garment on the actor, checking the fit around the neck and pin the leg and sleeve hems in place.

Measure the length of bias tape that is to cover the raw edge of the neck, adding two 16" lengths if a bias tie closing is to be used.

Stitch the bias tape to the neck.

Stitch the hems.

Press the hems.

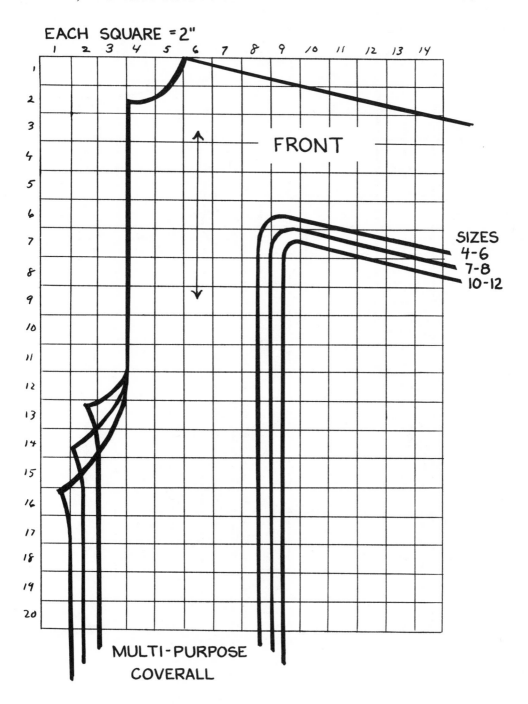

EACH SQUARE = 2"

FRONT

SIZES
4-6
7-8
10-12

MULTI-PURPOSE
COVERALL

**Figure 8-10**

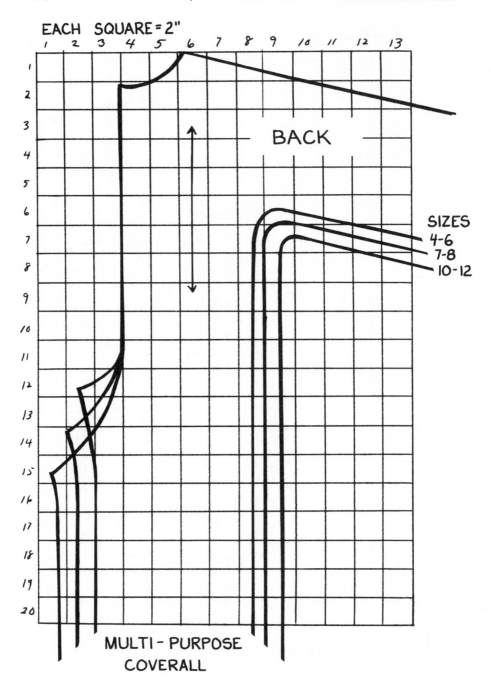

**Figure 8-11**

## THE MULTI-PURPOSE OVERBLOUSE

See Figures 8-4 and 8-12.

The amount of fabric needed is indicated below:

| Sizes 8 (small) | 10 (medium) | 12 (large) |
|---|---|---|
| 1 5/8 yds. 36" wide | 2 yds. 36" wide | 2 3/8 yds. 36" wide |
| 1 3/8 yds. 45" wide | 1 1/2 yds. 45" wide | 1 7/8 yds. 45" wide |

Before making the pattern, measure for individual sleeve and garment lengths, allowing 2" for hems.

**Procedure:**

Enlarge the grid pattern to scale as indicated in Figure 8-12.

Copy the pattern.

Cut out the pattern parts.

Fold the fabric so it is double and the selvages match.

Lay the pattern parts on the fabric and pin them in place, being sure you place the fold line of the patterns on the fold of the fabric.

Cut one front.

Cut one back.

Cut two sleeves.

Cut the front and back facings.

Stitch the front facing to the back facing at the shoulder line. This unit will be stitched to the garment later.

Press the facing seams open.

Pin the front and the back of the garment together with right sides facing each other.

Stitch the shoulder seams.

Press the shoulder seams open.

Turn the blouse right side out.

Place the right side of the facing unit on the right side of the blouse, fit the necks together as well as possible and pin them together. Stitch the facing unit the neck and front of the garment, following the stitching pattern as shown in Figure 8-12.

Trim the seam allowance around the neck to 1/4".

Using sharp scissors, cut a slash from the neck to the star as shown on the pattern front in Figure 8-12. Turn the facing to the inside of the garment press. Pin the sleeves to the front and the back of the garment and stitch as sown in Figure 8-13.

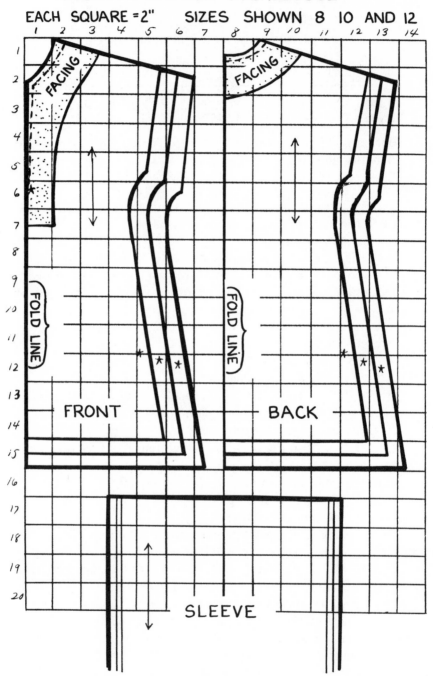

**Figure 8-12**

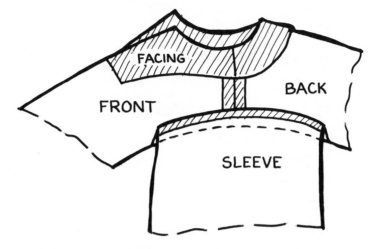

WRONG SIDE OF GARMENT

**Figure 8-13**

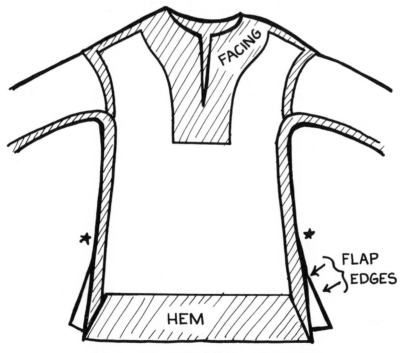

WRONG SIDE OF GARMENT

**Figure 8-14**

Stitch the side seams of the blouse beginning at the stars as shown in Figures 8-12 and 8-14.

Turn in the flap edges 5/8" and hem.

Hem the sleeves and the bottom of the garment.

Press the seams open and press the hems.

## THE MULTI-PURPOSE OVERBLOUSE . . . Long Version

See Figures 8-5 and 8-12.

The amount of fabric needed is indicated below:

| Sizes | | |
|---|---|---|
| 8 | 10 | 12 |
| 2 1/4 yds. 45" wide | 2 5/8 yds. 45" wide | 3 yds. 45" wide |

Before making the pattern, measure for individual sleeve and garment lengths, allowing 2" for hems.

**Procedure:**

Follow the sewing instructions for the Multi-Purpose Overblouse.

## THE BASIC LONG DRESS

See Figures 8-6 and 8-15.

The amount of fabric needed is indicated below:

| Sizes | | | |
|---|---|---|---|
| 8 | 10 | 12 | 14 |
| 3 5/8 yds. | 4 yds. | 4 1/2 yds. | 4 3/4 yds. 36" wide |
| 3 1/4 yds. | 3 7/8 yds. | 4 1/8 yds. | 4 1/4 yds. 45" wide |

**You Will Need:**

One 18" neckline zipper

Bias tape

Before making the pattern, measure for the length of the bodice from the nape of the actor's neck to her waistline. Measure for the length of the skirt and sleeves. Allow 2" for hems.

**Procedure:**

Enlarge the grid pattern to scale as indicated in Figure 8-15.

Copy the pattern.

Cut out the pattern parts.

Fold the fabric so it is double with the selvages matching.

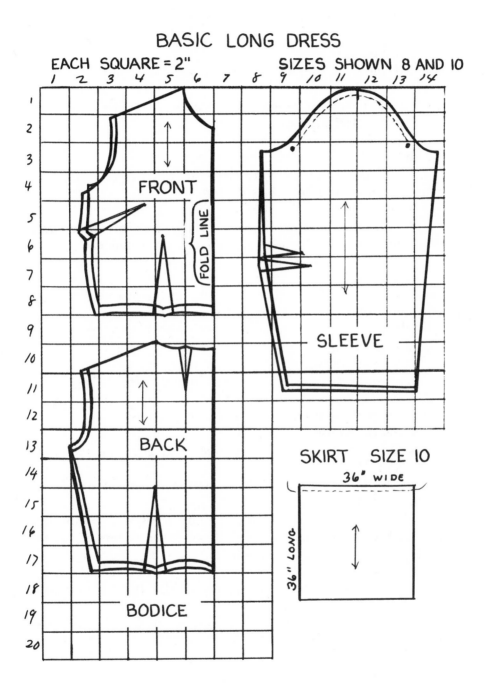

**Figure 8-15**

The front pattern is placed on the fold as indicated in Figure 8-15.

Cut one front.

Cut the two sides of the back (each facing in an opposite direction).

Cut two sleeves (each facing in an opposite direction).

Cut two skirt widths.

Mark all the darts with pins or lightly with a pen on the wrong side of the fabric.

Stitch the darts carefully, and tie the thread endings at the point into a knot to hold the stitching.

Press the darts flat.

Pin the front of the bodice to the back of the bodice, making sure that the right sides of the fabric are facing each other.

Stitch the front to the back beginning with the shoulder seams and then stitching the sides.

Sew a running stitch around the top of the sleeves, following the stitching plan shown in Figure 8-15.

Stitch the sleeve darts.

Press the darts flat.

Stitch each sleeve.

Place the right side of the sleeve armhole with the right side of the bodice armhole, ease the sleeve to fit the armhole of the bodice by pulling the running stitch of sleeve to size and pin.

Stitch the sleeves to the bodice.

Stitch a second time for reinforcement and trim the seam allowance to 1/4".

Stitch the sides of the skirt, leaving a part of one seam open where the zipper will be placed.

To determine the size of the opening, measure 18" from the bodice neck seam allowance of 5/8" down the back into the skirt, subtracting the waistline seam allowances.

Press the skirt seams open.

Sew a long machine stitch around the top of the skirt as shown in Figure 8-15.

Pull this running stitch into gathers that are eased into fitting the bodice around the waist.

Pin the skirt to the bodice.

Fit garment to actor.

Stitch the skirt to the bodice.

Stitch the neckline zipper into the garment, following the zipper manufacturer's instructions.

Check fit around the neck and then measure for the bias tape.

Stitch the bias tape over the raw edge of the neck.

Hem the sleeves and the skirt.

Press hems.

### A BOLERO AND VEST

See Figures 8-16 and 8-17.

**You Will Need:**

1/2 yd. of 36" wide fabric for all sizes.

Bias Tape.

Trimmings such as glitter, sequins, appliques, paint or fringe.

**Procedure:**

Enlarge the grid pattern to scale as indicated in Figure 8-17.

Copy the pattern.

Cut out the pattern parts.

Fold the fabric so that it is double with the selvages matching.

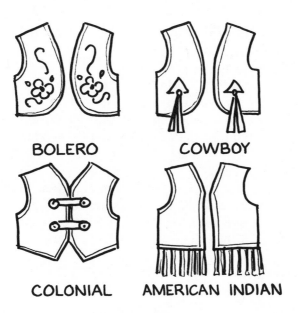

BOLERO          COWBOY

COLONIAL     AMERICAN INDIAN

**Figure 8-16**

The back pattern is placed on the fold as indicated in Figure 8-17.

Pin the pattern to the fabric and cut one back and two fronts.

Apply trimmings, except fringe, NOW—before stitching.

Stitch the shoulder seams.

Stitch the side seams.

Press the seams open.

Measure the raw edges, including the armholes, for the length of the bias tape which will cover these edges.

Stitch the bias tape to the garment.

Fringe can be stitched on at the same time you are stitching the tape.

Press the garment, but avoid pressing glitter, sequins, etc.

## THE PILGRIM CAP AND COLLAR—Dutch Cap and Collar

See Figures 8-18 and 8-19.

### You Will Need:

1-1/2 yds. of 36" wide fabric for the cap AND the collar
Bias tape.

### Procedure:

Enlarge the grid pattern to scale as indicated in Figure 8-18.

Copy the pattern.

Cut out the pattern parts.

Fold the fabric so that it is double—with the selvages matching.

Notice which patterns are required to be on the fold as indicated in Figure 8-18 and pin all pattern pieces in place.

Cut out the fabric—one crown and two brims.

Turn up a 1/4" hem along the bottom edge of the crown, stitch and gather slightly.

Pin the two pieces of the brim together, making sure that right sides of the pieces face each other on the inside.

Stitch where it is indicated in Figure 8-18. This will mean the longest side of the brim is not stitched at this time.

Turn the brim right side out.

Press the brim.

Pin ONE side of the brim to the right side of the crown. See Figure 8-19.

Stitch this brim side to the crown.

Bring the loose side of the brim over the raw edges of the crown and hand sew in place using a slip stitch. See Figure 8-19.

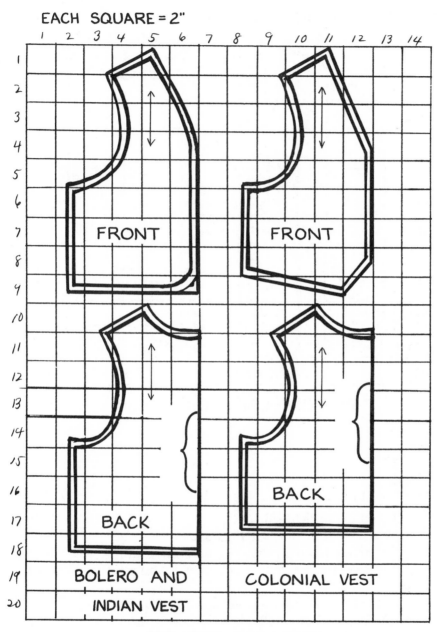

EACH SQUARE = 2"

FRONT

FRONT

BACK

BACK

BOLERO AND
INDIAN VEST

COLONIAL VEST

BOLERO AND VEST

SIZES SHOWN - 10 AND 12

**Figure 8-17**

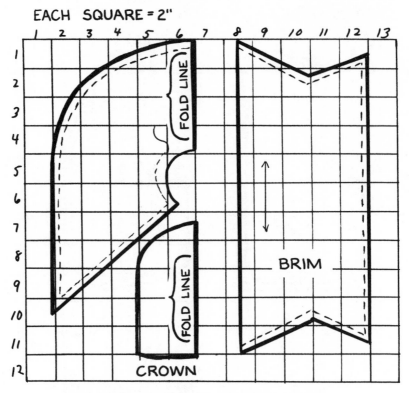

EACH SQUARE = 2"

PILGRIM COLLAR AND CAP

**Figure 8-18**

Turn the cap right side out.

Fold back the brim. See Figure 8-19.

For a Dutch cap effect, press the corners of the brim forward.

Add two 16" lengths of bias tape, if you want to tie it under the chin.

With the right sides pinned together, stitch the collar where it is indicated in Figure 8-18, thus leaving an open space for your hand to turn the collar right side out.

Turn the collar right side out.

Stitch the opening closed and press collar.

Add a tie of two 16" lengths of bias tape, or sew a snap fastening.

HEM AND GATHER • STITCH BRIM TO CROWN • SLIP STITCH

TURN BRIM  PILGRIM          DUTCH CAP

**Figure 8-19**

## THE PIONEER BONNET

See Figures 8-6, 8-20 and 8-21.

**You Will Need:**

5/8 yd. of 45" wide fabric

Nonwoven fabric like PELON for the brim interfacing

1 yd. of bias tape or 1" wide ribbon for the tie

**Procedure:**

Enlarge the grid pattern to scale as indicated in Figure 8-20. Copy the pattern.

Cut out the pattern parts.

Place the pattern on the fabric and pin in place.

Cut one crown.

Cut two brims.

Using the brim pattern, cut one brim interfacing from the nonwoven fabric.

Stitch around the crown with long machine stitches as shown in Figure 8-20.

Stitch at the base of the crown as shown in Figure 8-20 with long machine stitches.

EACH SQUARE = 2"

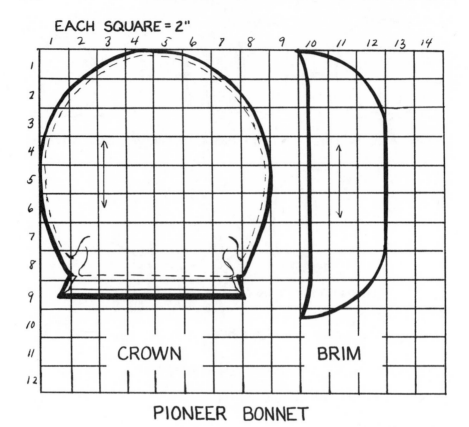

CROWN          BRIM

PIONEER BONNET

**Figure 8-20**

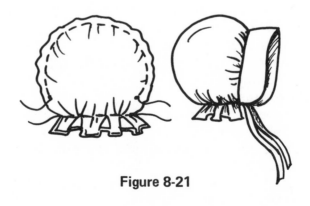

**Figure 8-21**

Stitch a 1/4" hem around the bottom of the crown on wrong side.

Make gathers around and at the base of the crown as shown in Figure 8-21.

Stitch the interfacing to one of the brim pieces.

Trim the interfacing to 1/4" away from the stitching.

With right sides together, pin and stitch the brim together leaving long side open.

Turn the brim right side out.

Stitch the open side of the brim together with long machine stitches.

With right sides together, pin the brim to the crown, easing gathers to fit the brim.

Stitch the brim to the crown.

Turn the bonnet right side out.

Sew the bonnet ties at the base of the brim.

### THE MULTI-PURPOSE CAP

See Figure 8-22.

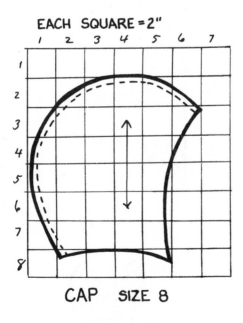

**Figure 8-22**

**You Will Need:**

    1/2 yd. of 36" wide fabric for all sizes

    Bias tape

**Procedure:**

    Enlarge the grid pattern to scale as indicated in Figure 8-22.

    Copy the pattern.

    Cut out the pattern part.

    Fold the fabric so it is double.

    Lay the pattern on the fabric and pin in place.

    Cut out the fabric.

    Stitch as indicated in Figure 8-22.

    Try the cap on the actor to check the fit.

    Clip the seam allowance so it is 1/4" away from the stitching.

    Press the seam open.

    Measure the raw edges for length of bias tape adding two 16" lengths for the under the chin ties.

    Stitch the bias tape to the cap.

    Add ears, antlers or any other decorations.

## THE COLONIAL MOBCAP

See Figures 8-6 and 8-23.

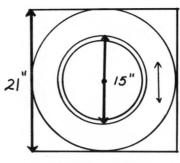

MOB CAP

**Figure 8-23**

**You Will Need:**

> 2/3 yd. of 36" wide fabric
> 1-1/3 yds. of 1/2" single fold bias tape
> 3/4 yd. of 1/4" elastic

**Procedure:**

To make your pattern, measure two concentric circles—one with a 21" diameter and the other with a 15" diameter. See Figure 8-23.

Cut out your two circle patterns.

Pin the larger circle pattern on the fabric.

Cut out the fabric.

Stitch a 5/8" hem around the perimeter of the circle.

Place the smaller circle pattern on the wrong side of the fabric and mark the circle with a pencil or pen.

Pin the bias tape on this line.

Stitch the bias tape along each of it's edges, thus making a tunnel for the elastic.

Thread the elastic through a bobby pin and pull it through the bias tape tunnel, adjusting the gathers.

Try the cap on the actor's head for correct fit and pin in place.

Sew the elastic ends together.

Sew the tape ends together.

## THE CAPE

See Figure 8-24.

**You Will Need:**

> Fabric
> Bias tape

Measure for the desired size and compute the yardage accordingly. Measure the length of the cape from the nape of the actor's neck. Compare your measurement with that of the pattern in Figure 8-24.

Enlarge the grid pattern to scale.

Copy the pattern.

Cut out the pattern.

Fold the fabric so it is double and place your pattern on the fold, IF your fabric is wide enough.

Cut two cape sides—each going in a different direction if the fabric is too narrow.

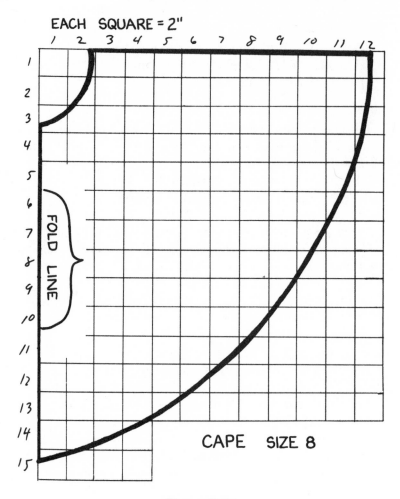

**Figure 8-24**

Stitch the two sides together and press the seam open.

Try the cape on the actor, checking the fit of the neck.

Measure the raw edges for length of the bias tape and include two 16" lengths for the tie closing.

Stitch the bias tape to the cape.

Press the cape.

## THE APRON

See Figures 8-6 and 8-25.

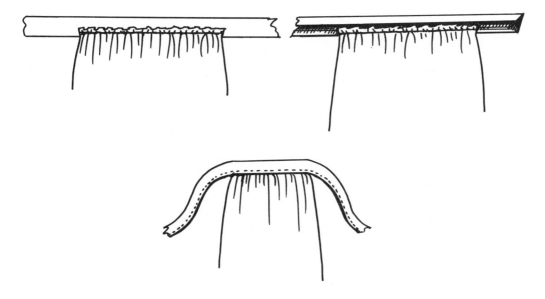

**Figure 8-25**

**You Will Need:**

    2/3 yd. of 36" wide fabric

    2 yds. 2" wide ribbon or hem facing for the ties.

**Procedure:**

    Stitch a 2" hem across one of the widths of the fabric. Hem the sides.

    Stitch with long machine stitches across the other width of the fabric.

    Pull this line of stitching into even gathers.

    Place your gathered fabric on the lower half of the ribbon or facing. The center of the fabric should match with half the length of the ties.

    Pin in place and stitch. See Figure 8-25.

    Turn the top half of the ribbon or facing over the raw edge of the fabric and pin in place.

    Stitch the ribbon or facing closed from one end of the tie to the other.

    Press the finished apron.

## THE BUSTLE

See Figures 8-6, 8-25 and 8-26.

### You Will Need:

2/3 yd. of 45" wide fabric

2 yards of 2" hem facing or ribbon

### Procedure:

Enlarge the grid pattern to scale as indicated in Figure 8-26.

Copy the pattern.

Cut out the pattern.

Fold the fabric so it is double and the selvages match.

Lay the pattern on the fabric, being sure that you place

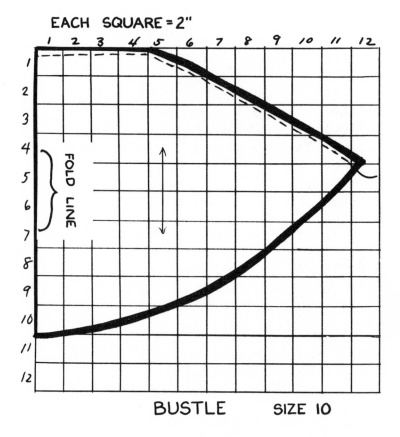

**Figure 8-26**

the fold line of the pattern on the fold line of the fabric as indicated in Figure 8-26 and pin.

Cut out the bustle.

Stitch a 3/8" hem along the bottom of the bustle.

Stitch long machine stitches along the top of the bustle as shown in Figure 8-26.

Pull this stitching to make gathers.

Fit these gathers to the actor's waistline and fasten the thread ends.

Pin the gathered bustle to the hem facing or ribbon as explained on page 153, making an apron as shown in Figure 8-25.

## THE VERSATILE TABARD

See Figures 8-7 and 8-27.

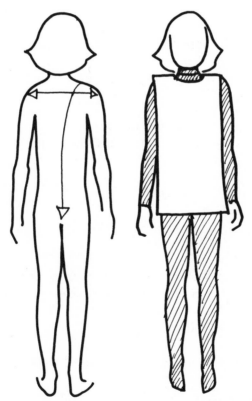

MEASURING FOR THE TABARD

**Figure 8-27**

**You Will Need:**

Fabric such as felt, heavy cotton or heavy paper

Decorations, appliques, paint, paper, etc.

You will have to compute your yardages after you have measured your actors.

**Procedure:**

Consult Figure 8-27 which shows how to measure the actor.

Measure the back—shoulder to shoulder for the width.

Measure the length by starting from the back crotch, continuing over the shoulder to the front crotch.

Cut out a 4-1/2" square from the center of the tabard for an opening that will pull over the head.

Stitch bias tape around the opening if fraying is a problem.

Apply decorations.

Keep the tabard from slipping by using double-faced tape on the actor's shoulders, chest and back.

Ties may be added at the waist on fabric tabards.

## SEWING TRICKS TO SPEED YOU ON YOUR WAY

### "Fur" Fabric

Look for remnants and save money.

Watch that all the nap goes the same way when placing pattern on the fabric.

Hand baste.

Use long machine stitch.

Slash the darts.

Do not use a steam iron on this kind of fabric.

### Felt

Felt, a non-woven fabric that comes in lively colors, looks well on stage. Since it has no grain, it can be laid out and cut in any direction.

The wide widths of 54" and 72" compensate for its cost per yard.

The leftover pieces can be used for glued on costume decorations or art projects.

Choose patterns with the least detail, so the felt can be easily managed.

Hemming is not needed.

Always press with a DRY iron.

### Rick-rack, Flat Braid, Bias Tape

Apply decorations on sleeves, skirt or pants before the garment is stitched together.

### Ruffles

Available ready-made.
Save money. Use hem facing or bias strips of left over fabric.
Use longest machine stitch and gather.

### Sequins

Mark sewing line, in chalk, on the finished garment's right side.

Fasten sequins by using a backstitch by hand.
Draw up thread so sequin lies flat.

### Fusible Tape and Webbing

Save time hemming and applying decorations by using these materials.
Follow the manufacturer's instructions.

### Velcro, a Tape Closure

Use instead of buttons, snaps, hooks and eyes and zippers.
Follow manufacturer's instructions.

### Zippers

Save time, use a self-basting zipper.
Use Scotch tape or basting tape to hold regular zipper in place while stitching.

### Bias Tape

Avoid making facings by using this type of finishing.
Finish garment, then measure for the amount needed.
Can be used for decoration, see "Rick-rack, Flat Braid, Bias Tape."


## SEVEN LUCKY SHORTCUTS TO
## SIMPLE "FUN" COSTUMING

1. Plastic dropcloths or leaf bags easily serve as capes, ponchos, Hawaiian hula skirts and African warrior skirts. They can be used for sashes and fringe.

Such plastic surfaces can be decorated with acrylic paint or Testor's enamels.

Cloth and paper designs may be glued to the plastic.

Use Mistik tape or masking tape on edges that may tear, such as the neck opening on a poncho.

2. Construction paper, even newspaper, is an excellent base for hats, headdresses and colonial wigs. See Chapter 9.

3. Cotton batting or polyester batting and terry towels make a good substitute for fur.

4. Colored sweatshirts as well as flannel and corduroy shirts give a fine imitation of velvet.

5. Berets supply a good base for many hat styles. Different type brims can be attached to them, as well as feathers and medallions.

6. Knee socks pulled up over long pants give the effect of the knee britches and hose of colonial times.

7. A regular boy's jacket, with each front side of the opening turned back at an angle and tacked, becomes a colonial-style jacket.

8. Paper bag masks and costumes.

## GUIDELINES FOR PRACTICAL MAKE-UP USE

Make-up is costuming too—and how your actors love it!

Play-acting is not only acting like someone else for a short time on a stage, it's looking like someone else too—and the right make-up well-applied helps with the illusion.

A certain amount of make-up is needed on everyone in the cast. Strong stage lighting drains life from the face so that even the most animated facial expressions appear dull and nondescript. Before using the make-up, refer to Chapter 7 under the heading— "Simple guidelines for color light planning.

Remember some of your actors may be allergic to certain kinds of make-up. For these actors, nonallergenic make-up, such as Almay is available. Otherwise, regular make-up purchased at any drug or variety store may be used. Professional type grease paint ought to be applied only by an experienced make-up artist. Avoid the use of spirit gum to attach mustaches and beards, since it may prove too abrasive on tender, acne-prone adolescent skin.

For hygienic reasons, insist that each actor bring and be responsible for his own towel and comb for his personal use at the pre-dress and dress rehearsals and the performance.

**Your Invaluable Make-up List**

1. Cold cream
2. Kleenex
3. Suntan liquid or pancake make-up base
4. Rachel liquid or pancake base
5. Suntan face powder
6. Rachel face powder
7. Rouge—dry or moist
8. Blue or green eye shadow
9. Brown eyebrow pencil
10. Liners—blue, brown, black and white
11. Powder brush
12. Baby powder, cornstarch, or bath talc
13. Q-tips
14. Cotton balls
15. Scissors
16. Towel

## MAKE-UP AN ACTOR IN SEVEN EASY STEPS

For the elementary grades, rouge and a little lipstick are all that is needed. Apply rouge high on the cheeks and blend smoothly toward the temples. The lipstick color should not be too intense especially for video presentations. When more elaborate make-up is required, the following method may be used.

1. Place towel around the neck to protect the costume.
2. Apply a little cold cream, then wipe it with tissue.
3. Smooth the suntan liquid or pancake make-up over the face and ears. Blend make-up with fingers to avoid that hard edge under the chin, and smooth around the nostrils. Hair-line blending is important. If a wig is worn, smooth the make-up into it.
4. Rouge the cheeks and blend toward the temples.
5. Make up the eyes by taking the dark brown or black liner and drawing a thin line along the edge of the upper lid from the inner corner of the eye to the outer corner and a little beyond. Blue liner or eye shadow is smoothed on the lid, above the eye and tapered off to the side. See Figure 8-28. If the eyebrows need darkening, use a brown liner or pencil on the hairs only. Avoid a hard line.

**Figure 8-28**

6. Dab face with a cotton ball which has some suntan powder on it. Smooth out the dabs with the powder brush. This will help maintain a matte finish on the face.

7. Remove make-up with lots of cold cream.

## SPEEDY CHARACTER MAKE-UP

Nobody wants wrinkles; that is, nobody except the student who has the important part of the old eccentric in the class play. Age wrinkles appear between the nostrils and mouth, at the outer corners and under the eyes, across the forehead and vertically between the eyes as illustrated in Figure 8-29.

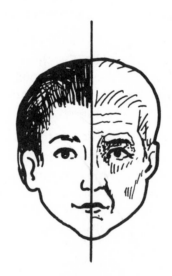

**Figure 8-29**

1. Apply rachel tone liquid or pancake make-up instead of suntan.

2. Indicate the wrinkle areas with a blue liner or eye shadow, using a Q-tip or similar applicator. With a white liner or

Max Factor's Erase, place white lines on either side of the blue line and blend.

3. The blue liner or eye shadow is used to make hollow cheeks. An unshaven chin will be blue with the addition of some black or brown liner or pencil.

4. Mustaches and beards are grown easily by drawing them with brown or black liners.

5. Gray or white hair is fashioned by using varying amounts of white bath talc or cornstarch. Don't forget to lighten the eyebrows with white liner.

Only minutes to curtain time! The players are in full costume. Such excitement! No peeking at the audience, please. Even "Thomas Jefferson" will be tempted to sneak a look from behind the curtain. However, illusion must begin even before the curtain rises.

After the final curtain, in the wake of the performance, the costume coordinator is there again to assist with the disrobing. She or he sees that the school-owned costumes are carefully taken off and stored, to provide a good costume base for future productions.

The coordinator should see that all borrowed or rented costumes and wigs are returned to the proper owners.

## Let's Review:

1. Research period plays.

2. Coordinate all parts of the costumes.

3. Use advancing colors on featured actors.

4. The costume coordinator contacts and sends pack to volunteers.

5. Keep make-up simple—just enough to enhance the personality of the character.

# CHAPTER 9

# Teacher-Tested Ways to
# Find and Make Props

Little Red Riding Hood enters left, carrying her basket of food. Slowly she walks to the bed in which Grandmother is tucked, "How are you, Grandmother?" she asks, "I've brought you some goodies." A familiar scene? Yes, with familiar characters and properties, or props. The basket of food is a hand prop; the bed is a stage prop.

## HAND PROPS. . . WHAT THEY ARE AND
## WHO IS RESPONSIBLE FOR THEM

Hand props are objects handled by the actors and fall into the following groups:

1. On-stage props—hand props placed by the prop crew on the set. (e.g., a telephone, a letter, a cup)

2. Off-stage props—hand props conveniently placed near entrances, where the actors can pick them up when entering a scene. (e.g., a tennis racket, a bouquet of flowers, a briefcase)

3. Personal props—hand props worn by the actor as part of the costume (e.g., a handkerchief, an eyeglass case, a wallet, a checkbook)

The actor obtains and is responsible for his personal props, which he should collect as soon as he receives his list from the prop manager.

## HOW YOUR PROP MANAGER CAN PLUNGE INTO FINDING STAGE PROPS

Stage props are furniture and other large objects used on the set. All props required by the script are listed in the director's book. Your prop manager should receive a copy of the list as well as a diagram for the stage prop placement from the director. He then determines the sources of these objects. Some props, hand or stage, which are not available from school equipment, can be gotten from pupils, friends, local drama groups, and local stores with the property manager's firm promise that all properties will be treated with the utmost care and returned in good condition promptly after the performance. Other props may have to be rented or made.

## HERE'S WHAT A PROP LAYOUT LOOKS LIKE IN YOUR DIRECTOR'S BOOK

Your play takes place in a vacation cabin. The stage layout of the furniture (stage props) in the director's book looks like this— See Figure 9-1.

The set is a simple interior, a sparsley furnished main room of a rustic vacation cabin, with two hassocks before the fireplace and three chairs around the one table.

The prop manager's prop list and the order of their use in the play follows:

1. Note is in fireplace for Peggy to find
2. Portable typewriter on upper right corner of table
3. 2 pieces of firewood in the woodbox
4. 2 canoe paddles against wall right of center back door
5. 1 fishing pole against wall left of door
6. 1 metal pail on floor left of center back door
7. 2 hassocks
8. 3 chairs
9. 1 table
10. 1 woodbox

All the furniture may be borrowed from a furniture merchant with the guarantee that his merchandise will be returned promptly in its original condition. The merchant's generosity will be graciously acknowledged in the program.

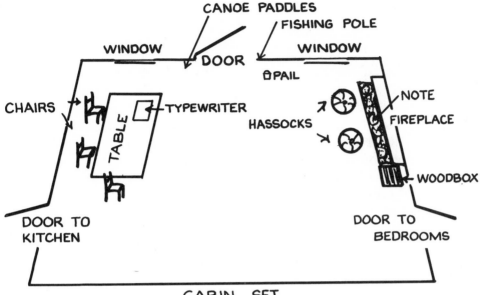

CABIN SET
SHOWING THE ARRANGEMENT OF FURNITURE
AS IT APPEARS IN THE DIRECTOR'S BOOK

**Figure 9-1**

## EASY WAYS TO HANDLE THE WHO, WHAT, WHERE OF PROP RESPONSIBILITIES

The prop manager and his crew collect and place props, except personal props, in their designated positions at rehearsals and the performance. If the number of props is small, one person can handle the job to avoid having people falling over each other. In general, it's wise to keep backstage personnel to a minimum.

All hand properties should be collected as soon as possible so the actors can rehearse with the real thing—a gun with blank cartridges, instead of a piece of wood; a ceramic mug, instead of a paper cup; a realistic treasure map, instead of a piece of newspaper. Using the actual prop helps the actors to get the feel of the situation and to get their timing down pat.

Additional props, not called for in the script, may be used to enhance the mood, tone and season of the scene—pots of geraniums for summer, overshoes by the door for winter, a silver candelabra on a table for elegance.

## THE PROP MANAGER'S METHOD FOR KEEPING A TIGHT PROP SCHEDULE

All hand and stage props should be assembled by rehearsal #13. Tag and place them in boxes which are clearly labeled as to act and scene.

While the property manager is collecting props, he must ask himself, "Is the color of this prop in keeping with the scenery? Does its style fit the period? Is it in good working condition? Can I make any changes on it? Is this prop large enough to be seen and identified by the audience? Will any flaws be noticeable to the audience?

Those props the property manager can't borrow or rent, he must *make*.

## TUNE INTO MAKING YOUR OWN PROPS WITH PAPIER-MÂCHÉ

Let's suppose you're doing a Thanksgiving play. In scene one the Pilgrims land on Plymouth Rock and your prop manager is faced with providing that impressive rock. In the fourth scene he needs a mouthwatering well-roasted turkey for the first Thanksgiving. Neither prop is available ready-made, so your stage crew makes these props by the following papier-mâché method of creating three-dimensional objects.

### PAPIER-MÂCHÉ

A method of making three-dimensional objects

**You Will Need:**

Plenty of newspaper or paper toweling, and the color comics of the Sunday paper
A piece of wooden board
Galvanized wire 1/8" diameter
Paste-flour or wallpaper paste (wheat paste)
Wire cutter
Pliers

**Procedure:**

1. Draw the design actual size.

2. Attach a long piece of wire to the board.

**Figure 9-2**

3. Bend the wires to shape. See Figure 9-2.

4. Make a paste of flour or wheat by adding enough water so the mixture is like thick pea soup.

5. Tear the paper into strips.

6. Wrap the strips which have been made wet with water and paste around the wire shape.

7. Interlock the strips where you can. See Figure 9-3.

8. Every other layer should be made with strips from the color comics so you can keep track of the layers.

9. After making several layers, let it dry.

10. Continue until you have six layers.

11. Let the prop dry naturally away from heat, which causes shrinkage.

12. If a smoother surface is desired, apply a thin coat of Spackle.

13. When the object is completely dry, paint, cover it with clear

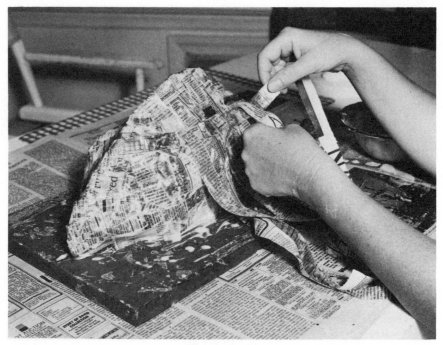

**Figure 9-3**

**Figure 9-4**

shellac or Krylon and add any three-dimensional details. See Figure 9-4.

You can make LARGE three-dimensional objects, such as Plymouth Rock, the jar in which Aladdin will hide, etc. Use this method:

1. Have all the supplies that are required for the smaller objects, but use 1" chicken wire instead of regular wire.
2. Clip off the finished edge of the chicken wire.
3. Interlock the cut ends of the chicken wire and bend to shape.
4. Follow the same paper and paste procedure as shown for smaller objects.
5. If drying is taking a long time, poke a few holes where least noticeable to let some air inside.
6. Paint with a broad bristle brush and avoid too many details.
7. Cover with clear shellac and add any three-dimensional decorations.

## 14 TRIED AND TRUE STEPS FOR MAKING SUCCESSFUL PAPIER-MÂCHÉ MASKS

**You Will Need:**

Plasticine (can be obtained through the school, at art stores and many candy stores)

Plenty of newspaper or paper toweling (be sure to include the Sunday comic section for color)

Paste—flour or wallpaper paste (wheat paste)

**Procedure:**

1. Draw outline to desired size and model the mask with plasticine. See Figure 9-5.
2. Make a paste of flour or wheat by adding enough water so the mixture is thick, like pea soup.
3. Tear the paper into strips.
4. Lay the wet strips on the modeled plasticine—NO paste on the first layer on the plasticine.
5. Interlock the strips where you can.
6. When the plasticine is fully covered, use *pasted* strips.
7. Alternate the paper layers with colored comics, which helps you keep track of layers. See Figure 9-6.

**Figure 9-5**

8. In all, make six layers of paper.

9. Let paper dry naturally away from heat.

10. The mask should be dry, or almost dry, before you lift it from the plasticine. (Too-wet paper can shrink.)

11. After the mask is removed, trim the ragged edges with scissors or an x-acto knife. Before the mask is painted, check that it fits well and the wearer can breathe and see without difficulty. If the holes for the eyes, nose or mouth need enlarging, cut these areas of the papier-mache gently with manicure scissors. When painting the mask, be careful to paint the inner rims of the eyes, nose and mouth so no light edges of paper show.

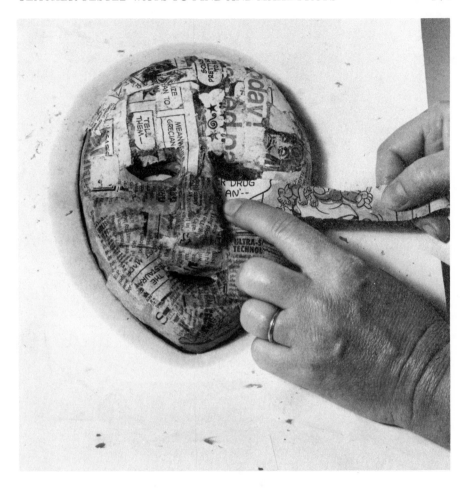

**Figure 9-6**

12. Paint with poster paint, acrylic or casein. If you are making an Eskimo or Alaskan Indian feather mask, you may want to use crepe paper for the feathers. These crepe paper feathers will have a richer look if applied to a prepainted base of the same color.

13. Coat the mask with clear shellac or Krylon.

14. Add three-dimensional details like yarn for hair, ornaments, glitter, fabric etc. See Figures 9-7a and 9-7b. Remember, do not paint minute details, which will be lost on stage. The mask's design should tell its story boldly.

**Figure 9-7a**

**Figure 9-7B**

## MAKE THAT HEADDRESS FIT WELL
## AND LOOK SENSATIONAL

Suggested uses, see Figure 9-8.

CHINESE
WOMAN'S
HEADDRESS

HAWAIIAN
CHIEF'S
HEADDRESS

COLONIAL LADY'S
'POWDERED' WIG

COLONIAL
MAN'S HAT

JAPANESE
LADY'S WIG

INDIAN CHIEF'S
HEADDRESS

ASTRONAUT'S
HELMET

GUARD'S
BUSBY

Figure 9-8

A simple base made of corrugated paper or oaktag is fashioned into a headband. Strips of paper are stapled to the headband. See Figure 9-9. These are covered with papier-mâche and painted or covered with crepe paper or construction paper. Additional materials such as yarn, feathers, jewels, mirrors, braids or anything imaginative can be glued to the headdress.

**Figure 9-9**

Remember headdresses must be worn with ease, fitting comfortably with no top-heavy feeling or pressure on the actor's head. Use a tie under the chin to solve slipping problems.

Furthermore, objects worn in the hair, such as ribbons, pom-poms and Spanish combs, must be attached securely and comfortably. Check these and the headdresses at the pre-dress rehearsal. The actors should not be distracted by their costumes—the need to adjust parts of the costume during the performance can be disconcerting not only to the actors, but to the audience.

### VENTURE INTO THE WORLD OF UNUSUAL STAGE PROPS MADE FROM ROLLED NEWSPAPER

Newspaper can be a very useful ally. It costs nothing, and is easily recycled into stage furniture.

Picture the scene where Alice in Wonderland has the problem of getting the key from a table that is higher than her reach. You create this outsized table, as well as the three different sized, but matching, furniture of the three bears, with rolled newspaper.

Add newspaper extensions to regular furniture, and create an entirely different look. Take an ordinary chair, tape your rolled newspaper to it, add any embellishments and you have a throne that certainly will dominate center stage.

Not only does newspaper solve the problem of making unusual furniture, but other kinds of props as well.  For example, Jack's beanstalk can be fashioned from rolled newspaper, so can George Washington's cherry tree, Lincoln's log cabin and split rail fence.  You can make a frontier stockade, a flag pole, a ship's mast, bed posts, birch and bamboo trees.

Follow these easy steps for making newspaper props:
(For table, stool and long lengths for poles, trees etc.)

**You Will Need:**

Plenty of newspapers
Masking tape
White glue
Paint
Heavy cardboard cut to desired size for table or stool surfaces.

**Procedure:**

1. Take six full sheets of newspaper, fold to page size, roll tightly and tape.

2. Use four of these rolls for each of the legs and tape together, adding white glue between the rolls for strength.

3. For a table-surface frame, make two rolls the length of the perimeter of the top of the table.  These will be *long rolls.* For long rolls, use this method:

    a. Overlap the narrower ends of five newspapers, See Figure 9-10

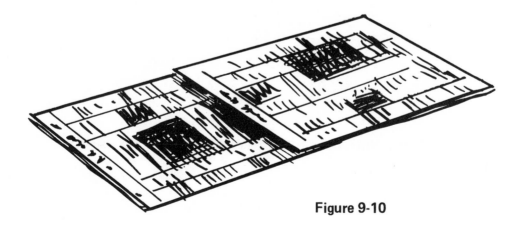

**Figure 9-10**

       b.  Tape in place, bringing tape around the edges.

       c.  Roll tightly and tape together.

4. Tape the two long rolls together, adding white glue between the rolls for strength.

5. Tape and glue the legs to the top frame.

6. Place double-face tape across the top. See Figure 9-11.

7. Carefully place the heavy cardboard table top on the frame and the tape.

8. Paint.

**Figure 9-11**

## HOW TO MAKE AN ORDINARY CHAIR INTO A THRONE

See Figure 9-12.

**Procedure:**

1. Take two long glued and taped rolls and tape them to a chair, curving them to size.

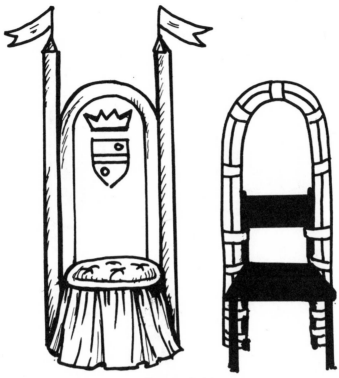

**Figure 9-12**

2. Add a long roll to either side of the curved back and tape in place.

3. Fill in the back of the throne with heavy cardboard glued to the newspaper frame.

4. Decorate with paint, add glitter and "jewels," a coat of arms.

5. Tape a ruffle to the chair seat, covering the legs.

6. Add a cushion.

Now that chair is fit for a king.

## TEN IDEAS TO LAUNCH YOU INTO MAKING SIMPLE, BUT EFFECTIVE, PROPS

See Figure 9-13.

1. Tape cut-out cardboard trees to corrugated boxes for support.

2. Make simple lanterns from milk cartons and one-quart Clorox bottles.

**Figure 9-13**

3. Stuff a brown paper bag with paper for a turkey. Apply a coat of shellac or clear Krylon spray for a nice shiny look.

4. Create a luscious-looking pie the same way, using brown paper for the crust and shellac or Krylon for shine.

5. Imitate the look of tapestry, paint your design on burlap.

6. Use large appliance packing cases to make small houses, caves, cabinets and wardrobes. Stack smaller corrugated boxes from the supermarket for chairs.

7. Produce a tepee base: acquire a stepladder and cover with paper or fabric.

8. Make rounded objects, such as crowns, out of corrugated paper which bends easily.

9. Paint a plunger gold, add a banner and ribbons for that royal look.

10. Place a real tree branch in a bucket of sand, tape on paper leaves for more realism.

Additional ideas and directions for making props, masks and headdresses for the elementary grades are to be found in the book, *Art Today and Every Day* by Jenean Romberg and Miriam Rutz, published by Parker Publishing Company.

## CLEVER SOLUTIONS TO THREE BIG PROP PROBLEMS

1. Do not permit the use on stage of any object with a flame. Daniel Boone's campfire should be a light bulb or flashlight covered with plastic gel or cellophane; Paul Revere's lantern can hold a Cyalume glowing light stick, made by American Cyanamid. This "cold light" is safe and effective.

2. Do not permit smoking on stage. Put talc in Sherlock Holmes' pipe and the actor can gently blow out the talc for a smoking effect.

3. Do not permit eating or the drinking of carbonated beverages on stage. It can interfere with the actor's diction, or may cause him to cough, choke, hiccough or burp. Snow White must *pretend* to bite the apple.

Use the following for realistic prop food:

| | | |
|---|---|---|
| Fried eggs | —— | Peach halves |
| Meat | —— | Purple plums |
| Bacon strips | —— | Curled up, dried apple parings |
| Amber-colored drinks | —— | Tea in glasses |

It is time for the pre-dress rehearsal; from now on everything is GO. The mirror is on the wall for Snow White's stepmother's reflection, Sir Walter Raleigh's cape is ready to be placed before Queen Bess, the sword is in the rock, waiting for King Arthur's mighty tug, Edison's electric light bulb is ready to light on cue.

## Let's Review:

1. Use actual hand and personal props as soon as possible.

2. All stage props are to be in position for the pre-dress rehearsal.

3. After the performance, return all borrowed or rented props promptly and in good condition.

4. Store props that are school property for future use.

# CHAPTER 10

# Creating a Fantasy World
# With Special Effects

"We perform our tricks in various ways," says Mr. Wechsler, lighting director of the Metropolitan Opera House, talking about special effects in *The New York Times*. "Of course, certain effects create problems." Like Gil Wechsler, you will be performing tricks, visual and audio, and you will have your problems. Suggestions in this chapter will help you create effects with a minimum of fuss. Don't hesitate to ask your class for suggestions for solving some of the problems. They may have worked on a similar setup in school or in scouting. Or you may have some pupils who are especially inventive and imaginative who would like working on this type of project. It would provide them with an opportunity to work on novel solutions and would add immeasurably to their learning experience.

## WHY TEMPLATES GIVE YOU MAXIMUM RESULTS

Continuing with the theme of lighting from the previous chapter, here is information concerning special effects with the use of templates with designs on them. Ellipsoidal spots with templates have been used since the 18th century. A large selection of these templates is offered by Time Square Theatrical and Studio Supply Corporation. For catalogs of special effects systems, write:

Times Square Theatrical and Studio Supply Corporation
318 W. 47th Street
New York, New York 10036    (212) 245-4155

If you would like to make your own templates; here's what you do:

1. Draw your design on white paper. Make the size of this design the same as the acetate filters or those you have made for your Kodak Carousel. See Chapter 7.

2. Place the acetate filter over the design.

3. Paint the design on the acetate with *acrylic* paint, used like opaque or water colors. You can also cut out acetate silhouettes and carefully cement them to the filter.

## A DIRECTOR'S GUIDE TO EXCITING VISUAL EFFECTS SYSTEMS

Science fiction, fantasy, a disco setting, Fourth of July—all lend their themes for a great opportunity to use visual effects. The Edmund Scientific Company, 1776 Edscorp Building, Barrington, New Jersey 08007, can supply your school with a visual effects system that can provide such spectacular color moving shows as:

| | |
|---|---|
| rippling color | starburst |
| fire effect | whirling rods |
| 3-D geometrics | colored clouds |
| colliding planets | swirling cycloids |
| kaleidoscope | musical notes |
| bubbles | windows |
| psychedelics | moving colors |
| stars | |

These effects are produced by using these wheels of various designs with a three-way kaleidoscope lens that can be used on any projector. The descriptions of the wheels and other accessories are as follows:

1. Psychedelic wheel—Can be used with any accessory wheel.

2. Hexidoscope—Is a 5" tube with six front-surface mirrors placed hexagonally on the inside for semikaleidoscope effects.

3. Colored window wheel—Random colored windows with opaque backgrounds. Can be used with any accessory.

4. Colored clouds—6" mylar-lined tube.

5. Lenticular wheel—Usually used with a 12 rpm motor. When spinning in front of the projection lens, with another wheel, it can produce a wild whirling and turning effect.

6. Striped wheel—This has 12 strips in six colors. It can be used with any other accessory.

7. Window wheel—Same as the colored window wheel, except the round windows are clear, but can be painted, decorated with plastic, etc.

8. Musical note wheel—This includes hundreds of notes.

9. Bubble wheel—This type wheel is filled with liquid. The bubbles ooze and flow between the layers of colored plastic.

10. Three-dimensional wheel—A lenticular wheel used with this wheel will produce moving three-dimensional effects.

Is anyone on the lighting staff eager to try and make a color wheel? Edmund Scientific Company also sells 9" discs of either glass or plastic to the person who wants a special color, kaleidoscopic or general image projection.

## MAKE A GHOST APPEAR WITH LIGHTING MAGIC

Lighting can become your "magic" touch when it comes to making a ghost appear and then disappear. If your ghost isn't required to be in motion, a special effect can be accomplished by the use of particular lighting and color. Where you want the ghost to appear, you paint it's outline in orange. When you want it to appear, throw a blue light in it's direction and the outline will stand out boldly. If you use this method, the "ghost" should appear in a rather obscure, dimly lit part of the stage.

You can also paint a ghostly outline with blacklight paint and bring the outline into view by shining an ultraviolet light on it.

When the script demands that the "ghost" move about, it means an actor will be performing in a suitable environment.

Magicians have been accomplishing that special effect on stages for many years, and the following instructions will tell you how to make this type of scenery. See Chapter 6 on scenery, where this effect is in the planning stage. This section, the effect, must fit inside the dimensions of one flat.

**Procedure:**

1. Select a suitable place where the apparition is to appear (check script for details); the place might be a bookcase. See Figure 10-1.

**Figure 10-1**

2. Do not paint any scenery on that particular canvas area because you will cut out that area.

3. Glue theatrical gauze to the cut-out area of the flat, keeping it very taut.

4. Now that the gauze covers the cut-out area, paint the design that would ordinarily be on the canvas on the gauze.

5. A solid black drop will be placed behind your gauze area, leaving room for the actor's moving about. See Figure 10-2.

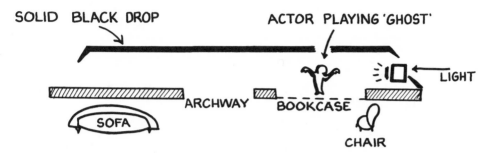

TOP VIEW OF 'GHOST' SET

**Figure 10-2**

6. A spotlight is placed as shown in Figure 10-2.

7. At performance time your "ghost" will appear and disappear on cue because your lighting crew will:

   a. Darken the stage lights.

   b. Throw the spot on the figure.

   c. Bring stage lights back up.

The "ghost" is seen through the gauze when the lights are down. When the lights are up, the scenery that is painted on the gauze looks the same as that painted on the canvas.

## FIVE FIRELIGHT EFFECTS AND HOW
## TO ACHIEVE THEM

Very often "lighted" fireplaces and campfires are required or desired in the play. Instructions on how to accomplish various fire effects follows:

### Fireplace

A fireplace on a side wall, mentioned in Chapter 7, throws out a warm glow on the surrounding furniture because spotlights with red and amber filters provide this certain look. However, the spots must be placed low and out of sight.

### Fire in Grate

This grate glow can be simulated by filling the grate with logs or papier-mâché "coals" covered with red and amber cellophane or plastic. A light (usually a flashlight) is placed at a safe distance under the props in the grate.

### Campfire

Use the same method as above, only pile the sticks into a pyramid shape like a real campfire.

### Dancing Flames Fire

Employ color wheels that have been described earlier in the chapter.

### Smoke

Use dry ice.

## SEVEN ATTENTION-GETTING WEATHER EFFECTS

Continuing with the visual aspects of your play, showing weather conditions may be important. Here are some of the ways that "weather" can be realistically presented:

### Lightning

Use electronic camera flash bulbs, especially when repeat flashes are needed.

### Falling Snow

Cut up white paper into bits and throw the paper into the path of air produced by a fan.

### Fallen Snow

Dampened salt can be applied where needed. When an actor must come stamping inside, covered with snow, use this method. He can brush the salt off easily and when the salt flies in the air, it really looks like powdery snow.

Place cotton batting where you want the illusion of snow depth on the ground, window sills, etc.

### Rain

Showing rain is very tricky and best not attempted. Also the use of flowing water around electrical wiring is dangerous.

### Sunlight

Sunlight streaming through a window is achieved by placing a large spotlight off stage. Use amber filters which will be lighter or darker depending on the time of day.

### Moon

Cut out the phase of the moon you want out of cardboard, and attach it to a cloth backdrop or cyclorama. Place a spotlight behind the cloth and direct its beam on the cutout.

### Stars

String Christmas lights behind a dark blue gauze or scrim.

Now, when your plays calls for some audio clues to the weather outside, you can use some of the following suggestions.

### Thunder

Hang a metal sheet backstage. Shake or strike it for the desired effect.

### Wind

There are machines that can be rented for this purpose.

### Rain

Shake dried peas or beads in a box or you can drop them on a drum. If the downfall of rain is to continue for some time; set the box of peas or beans on a rocker.

## EASY IMITATIONS OF COMMON SOUNDS

The following list includes common sounds that are required to be heard in many plays:

### A Crash

Drop a closed sack filled with fragments of rocks, metal, glass, etc.

The dropping of this sack offstage will provide the surprising sound you want.

### Door Chime

A real front door chime may be borrowed from a hardware store. If this cannot be done, use an xylophone.

### Telephone

Connect a real electrical bell or use an alarm clock.

If two or more jangling sounds are to be used during the play, make sure they make different sounds.

## HOW TO USE A TAPE RECORDER FOR SENSATIONAL SOUND EFFECTS

Need the sound of a barreling freight train? How about the hoot of a Mississippi steam boat? Just about any sound has been recorded by someone, and many of them are available on special order from local record stores. It may take a while to get them, so order well enough in advance of your production date.

Playing a record can be a mite clumsy when you are trying to keep actors on cue, and the props from falling down. By far, the best way to handle these special sound effects is with a tape recorder. A small recorder can be used to record any of the sounds that are available on the records, and you can even mix a number of sounds to get the special effect that gives your play that perfect mood. But, there is a trick to this that we will explain later.

You can use a small tape recorder if your audience is small and the hall is too. Don't try to use such a recorder in any room larger than the average classroom. For an auditorium, you should plan to use the output of a small recorder fed into the auditorium sound system, or set up a P.A. system that will handle the space. Large systems use reel-to-reel tape systems; that is, the tape is on larger reels that must be threaded between the recording heads and the other guides. A cassette recorder has both reels in a self-contained package, and it's just a matter of plopping the cassette in the recorder and pushing the right buttons.

Because there are so many different types of reel-to-reel and cassette systems, it is all but impossible to give specific instructions for their operation here. But, if you have the instruction booklets that came with the equipment, or can locate one of your students with an interest in electronics or ham radio, you will have little trouble with the equipment. More often than not, the industrial arts instructor can do the job, too.

Tape recorders pick up sound from a microphone that is either integral with the recorder or is separate, but plugs into the unit by way of a long cord. Other more elaborate systems may have input connections for other equipment such as radios and record players. Discover which way yours works, and familiarize yourself with the controls before you begin making your tapes for the play. Most tape equipment is pretty basic once you understand the operation.

Now, let's suppose that you need the sound of a train and the sound of a thunder storm at the same time. Records of both can be ordered from specialty recording houses, but the problem is to get both sounds on the same tape. At first, you may think that it is possible to record the train first and then superimpose the sound of the thunder storm on a second pass. This can be done only with very expensive and sophisticated equipment. Most of the sound equipment found in schools is set up so that as the head records, it wipes out what was previously recorded on the tape. So, if you lay down the train, and then try to superimpose the storm, all you will have is the storm. But, all is not lost.

With two or more record players going simultaneously, you can do the job with a single tape. However, this will take a few practice runs before you will hit the right spots and timing on both recordings to get the sound imposition you want. The best way to do this is with a stop watch for each recorder. Time, to the second, the appearance and disappearance of the sounds you want to put on each tape. When you start both recordings at the same time, ride the gain, or volume controls to eliminate sounds you don't want until the watch says it's time. You may want to fade it in and out gradually, or hit it hard, depending on what the sound is to accomplish.

If holding two or more stop watches, twirling the volume controls on several record players and cueing a tape recorder sounds like a job for an octopus, you are right. But, it's still a simple matter, if you have help. You can actually create a script, and have your student helpers time the records and run up the gain when the appropriate sound is to be recorded. If you are smart, you will write yourself a conductor's score so that you can cue in your helpers. It's not unlike leading an orchestra. It's not just a matter of cueing in the right recorder, you want to have each player produce the sound at the right level for your composite soundtrack.

It will probably take several tries before you get the tape you want, but it will be well worth it when you think of the alternatives.

Now that you have your sound background recorded and timed, you must have a few run-throughs with your actors. If the action is too slow or fast for the soundtrack, you will have to either make a new track, or change the action of the play sufficiently to follow the sound. Once the players become accustomed to the pace of the sound, there should be no problems.

Be sure that your sound effects person has a cue sheet and has each sound sequence properly cued to the action of the play, as mentioned earlier. Many tape systems include a digital counter to indicate where different parts of the recording are placed. When each sound segment is identified and keyed to the sound-person's sheet, all that is required is to advance the recorder to the appropriate number before the next sound is to be played.

Be sure to test the level of your recorder output before the play. Can it be heard at the back of the room? Can the little sounds that announce spooky events be heard by everyone without sounding like a trumpet quartet? A squeaky door, heard well in the back of the room, may sound like the building is coming down in the front row. Moderate and modulate—test the sound until there is no mistaking what it is and what it is supposed to mean. Remember that sounds set the mood, but you can break it with too much. Kids like a lot of noise, but when they know what the sound is supposed to accomplish, they will control the amplitude appropriately.

Your play may not end with a spectacular lightning display with full thunder accompaniment like the presentation of Rigoletto at the Metropolitan Opera House, however, your play can provide successful visual effects and sound effects, pleasing both audience and crew.

## Let's Review:

1. Consult the script for directions that call for special effects.
2. Make and distribute cue sheets for the lighting and sound effects crew.
3. Plan to borrow or purchase needed equipment.
4. Experiment with the equipment as early as possible.
5. Be sure the crews are familar with the cues before the thirteenth rehearsal—the light rehearsal.

CHAPTER **11**

# Moment of Glory—How to
# Succeed on Opening Night

At last, the twentieth day on your schedule—the day of the performance!

It's just a bit more than 60 minutes to curtain time, when this show you've worked so hard to put on plays before its ultimate judge—the audience. Let two-thirds of that audience (a commercial play's best hope) applaud and laugh in all the expected places, let the players react to that applause and laughter with "That was fun! Let's do it again," and your production's an instant hit. After all, a successful play is created by the mutual efforts of both audience and players.

## YOUR PLACE IS BACKSTAGE

Now, contrary to all other advice you read or receive about making yourself scarce backstage during this hour before curtain time and about sitting in the audience taking notes on weak spots during the performance, stick around backstage, right through curtain calls, in full view of your cast and crew. You've been and still are the buoyant heart of the production. Be there; help to meet last-minute problems; smile encouragement and warmhearted approval.

What you do and say, and what problems arise, however, vary with the show you're doing.

191

## DETAILED RUN-DOWN ON YOUR ACTIVITIES
## DURING THE LAST 60 MINUTES
## BEFORE CURTAIN TIME

### 1. Lower School Cast Presenting Creative Dramatics on an Open Stage

If your seven and eight-year-old players are staging an afternoon performance of their creative version of the nursery rhyme, "The Queen of Hearts/ She Made Some Tarts," for the rest of the lower school:

*60 Minutes to Curtain Time:* You're probably supervising the seating arrangements for a wiggly, usually noisily responsive audience. This multi-purpose room you're calling the theatre today serves the school as gymnasium, lunch room and assembly hall. At one end there's an elevated picture-frame stage with a curtain, but you've chosen to use an open stage or three-quarter arena stage (See Chapter 5.)—a stage area with one side as background and with the audience equally distributed on the three other sides. Your stage is the floor in front of the raised stage. Three-paneled screens range across the back and extend R and L to form wings. You've made this choice because young players on an open stage achieve greater rapport with their audience than young players on a picture-frame stage. They're more easily heard and seen, and a young audience, such as this afternoon's, enjoys the intimacy and immediacy of this staging arrangement. "It's like being in the play," children say.

The lack of a curtain doesn't matter either, especially since your set is simple, requiring no changing or shifting of scenery. The audience will fill in any blanks with their imagination. Just be sure lines of the actors reveal where they are at all times.

For the audience that you're expecting, you'll reserve floor space on three sides of the playing area, since most of them will squat cross-legged on cushions from their own classrooms, exercise mats from the gymnasium cupboards, hand-made sit-upons (if a supply is available) or on the bare floor.

A "sit-upon" is just what it says, a mat to sit upon, durable and moisture-proof for use indoors or out. It is made by layering squares of newspaper (18" X 18") to 3/4" to 1" thickness, and covering the paper with squares of oilcloth or vinyl or plastic-covered fabric (18½" X 18½"). The extra 1/2" is allowed for blanket-stitching the fabric together with worsted. This is a good handcraft project for boys and girls interested in making something useful for their school.

A seating arrangement like this cuts down on the noise that a lively young audience generates just by its presence, for there's little jumping up and down and no creaking of moveable chairs. You'll set up, with the help of the custodian, of course, folding chairs on the three open sides of the stage beyond the children's seating area for adults (relatives, friends, teachers).

Your theatre plan and set take this shape:

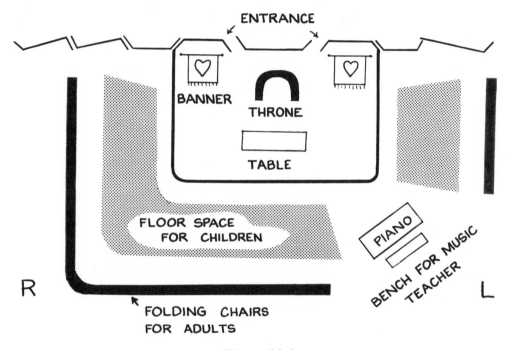

**Figure 11-1**

You are using a minimum of essential stage and hand props— table, throne, royal coat of arms (large cut-out hearts) on banners attached to screens U R and U L, tarts on a cookie sheet. The costumes are garments made by mothers in the colors and materials you requested, and gold-paper crowns (See Chapter 9 for instructions.) for all players (Everyone wanted to wear a crown, and why not?). The only lighting is the natural daylight coming through the over-sized windows on the outside wall of your theatre.

So your stage is set and the seating arrangements are complete just as the school bell buzzes across the playground, summoning the pupils back to class after the lunch recess.

*55 Minutes to Curtain Time* (**C.T.**): You're in your own classroom with your young players and one or two mothers who are helping the players to dress and are applying to eager, upturned faces the slightest touch of rouge to lips and cheeks and maybe a tracing of eyebrow pencil. If you're a purist, don't use make-up, for it really isn't needed today, but the players love it. It's part of being in a play, being different—being an actor.

Every child in the class has a part, for you've written in a chorus with some simple lyrics for them to sing—a chorus of crowned princes and princesses to take care of all the pupils without speaking parts. For a finale to the playlet you may even have worked out a lively dance routine for the chorus in the Elizabethan tradition of the jig at the end to send the audience away in a jolly mood.

The mechanics of these musical additions are simple:

1. For the song, work with the music teacher. Use a tune familiar to the pupils and be sure to rhyme the short, easy-to-remember lyrics. Repeated rendition of the same lines of the song so that the audience can join in after a while is better than a long song.

2. For the dance, work again with the music teacher and also with the physical education teacher, whose teaching repertoire includes dancing of the type you want—folk and set dancing. (Assign two of the onstage crowned chorus to shift the table on the set D C to U L to allow more stage area for the dancing.)

*25 Minutes to C.T.:* Everything's under control—no tears, no jitters, no problems. So far, so good.

*20 Minutes to C.T.:* You make a last check-up of the set and suddenly realize the tarts are startingly conspicuous by their absence. No tarts, no show. You double-time it back to your classroom, clutching the empty cookie tray.

"Lucy," you say to the Queen of Hearts, whose pregnant mother had begged off on helping backstage this time and volunteered to bring the tarts on the day of the performance, "did Mother mention the tarts this morning?"

"Yes," Lucy nods, royally aware of the dignity of her queenship. "Mother's bringing them when she comes to see our play with Martin's mother."

"My mom's here," flips Martin. (He's the knave.) "I looked, and your mother's not with her, Lucy."

*15 Minutes to C.T.:* You can hear the lower school classes moving through the corridors. You know that a goodly number of guests who expect a good show are already seated. Your shows are always good. They remember the last–"Around the World with Cookie Monster"–a smash! Of course, that time it wasn't tarts but the grass skirt of a hula dancer that mysteriously disappeared. When 10 minutes to C.T. a frantic search failed to produce the skirt, you solved the problem by improvising. You shredded packets of crepe paper, supplied by an understanding art teacher, stapled them to an old venetian blind tape, supplied by the "good-old" custodian, and encircled your hula dancer with these copious undulating fringes seconds before her entrance, and eased her onstage on cue.

There's always something. This time no tarts. (You must improvise again.)

Queen Lucy's face begins to crumple, threatening tears to stain her pretty costume and streak her make-up.

A hurried conference with the kindergarten teacher ensues. There's some fast handwork with play-dough, and presto–a batch of pretend-tarts graces the cookie tray just as your principal's secretary whispers a message for you from Lucy's father.

Presently as you usher the players from classroom to stage wings, you smile at Lucy, whose own smile is now all-encompassing. She knows that even if she has to make-do with make-believe tarts in the play, it's a new baby brother she has for real.

*C.T.:* Everything's ready. Allowing the audience no opportunity to get restless and noisy, you signal the music teacher, whose hands are poised over the keyboard of her piano. She strikes several arresting chords, following them up with a thrilling attention-catching run of lively notes to produce a hiatus of expectant hush. The costumed prologue enters U R, moves D C and welcomes the audience and announces the play. (You've wisely eliminated programs, for young children don't care about reading them anyway.) Prologue now bows graciously and exits U R. It's now M for MOMENT–the magic moment of anticipation, that pre-play hush when hearts beat high and hard (yours too!) And the play begins.

What do you do now? During most of the performance you remain backstage, engineering entrances, prompting lines (You know the simple script so well you don't need your director's book.), and greeting players on their exits with smiles and hugs of approval.

At last when all your actors, including the royal chorus, are on stage for the grand finale, you join the audience. When the last word has been uttered, the last song has been sung, the last dance step has been danced, and when the players bow to the audience, you lead the applause.

Young audiences are usually ready enough with their laughter during the play, sometimes even adding bits of original dialog to the play themselves, but often they have to be shown how to respond to a live play when it's over. So show them. This is the teacher in you taking charge.

Show them by applauding heartily yourself. Imitate someone whose behavior the children will recognize—the TV emcee, who gestures encouragingly toward the audience for more applause for the performers.

Accustomed to viewing TV and movie house films, the young playgoer doesn't realize how sweet and necessary the music of applause is to even the youngest actors.

Once these playgoers catch on, they're delighted to do what is expected of them. Now delight them further. Turn the trick on them. Gesture for the players to applaud their appreciative audience. Lead this applause yourself. The audience will love it.

All that remains now is a fast exit and the cleanup.

The custodian (a teacher-director's best friend) will strike the set after the players and the audience have left, store the mats and the three-paneled screens, and stack the folding chairs. Bless him!

You, having repossessed the pretend-tarts, marshall your players off stage through exits U R and U L back to your classroom. There you rescue for storage any costume parts that belong to the school's play wardrobe. You return the play-dough to the kindergarten and the cookie tray to the cooking room.

When the dismissal bell rings, as it does shortly, you send your players home in costume and make-up (You probably can't get them to remove either at this point.) with their gold-paper crowns as souvenirs of the afternoon's fun.

Then as your players fade into the sunset, you slowly sink into your chair, put your feet up, and relax. Further thank-you's can wait. This is a magic moment for you. Relish it.

### 2. Juniors or Young Adults Staging a Full-Length Mystery-Comedy on a Picture-Frame Stage

On the other hand, if your junior or young adult players are staging the performance of a full-length mystery-comedy for a paying audience:

*60 Minutes to C.T.:* You are in the lobby of your theatre, the school auditorium this time with a picture-frame stage (or proscenium stage that has a proscenium arch, a curtain, etc. See Chapter 5.) With a trained teacher's peripheral glance, you take in everything–the prompter, staff list in hand, checking off cast and crew arrivals; the security officer on duty discussing with the custodian the extent of the area he is to patrol. You pick up a program. Several stacks of them lie neatly arranged beside the ticket-stub receptacle on the ticket-taker's table. Other tables and chairs, one for "box office" and one or more for the vendors, in this case a girls' service club, have been set out by the custodian.

The program is happily correct in every detail even to the unusual spelling of the composer's name for one of the numbers the school orchestra is playing between the two acts. You tuck the program into your director's book and go down the side aisle of the threatre for a last check of the house. The lights are on. Doors are open. You mount the side steps to the stage apron. Suddenly the curtain parts, revealing a modern set–the book-filled study in the country house of a mystery-story writer. One head, then a second pops into view around the edge of the curtain R–your stage manager's and your special effects supervisor's.

"Sorry, Boss. Didn't know you were there." Your stage manager grins at you. "Just testing. Don't want the curtain to stick the way it did at dress rehearsal."

You nod your approval. Effects supervisor flashes you a distress signal. He has something on his mind. You'll need to check this out. At the moment, however, you're glad the curtain stuck at dress rehearsal, leaving ample time before the performance for the school's custodian to repair it. That's what dress rehearsals are for–to iron out the rough spots.

At that, your dress rehearsal came off fairly well because both your cast and stage crews are mutually responsive and geared from their past weeks of hard work under your direction to know their jobs and how to do them. That fallacious old bromide *Bad dress rehearsal, good performance* and its converse *Good dress rehearsal, bad performance* just won't wash. True, your dress rehearsal was less than inspired, but you know that come performance time, with a live audience on the other side of the footlights, something special happens–theatre magic takes over.

*55 Minutes to C.T.:* You step onto the set, and the stage manager closes the curtain. Effects supervisor is beside you pouring out his problem: "That block and tackle I rigged to hoist the phosphorescent head up and down, behind the U L window in the First Act when the lights dim, won't work. Rope's snapped. No way I can get in to repair it. . . No room. We've got to squeeze in a small-sized, and I mean 'small,' head-holder back there to work the head by hand."

You agree, but who is there? The effects man himself doesn't meet that requirement. Hasn't since he was 11. Popping your own heads through the window, which is a working stage prop, the two of you inspect the limited space available. *Small* is right.

*50 Minutes to C.T.:* The prompter joins you to report, "All cast and crew members are aboard except. . ." You hold your breath. . . "one of the props people. . . a skateboard accident, but the property manager has brought his little sister. She looks as though she thinks he's Superman. She'll do exactly what her brother tells her—her brother promises."

His little sister!

Effects supervisor breaks in. "His little sister? Hey, where is she? Maybe she'll fit." And his space problem is solved.

*45 Minutes to C.T.:* You're backstage now. It's an anthill of "busyness." The atmosphere hums with high expectancy. Some of the players are dressing; others are waiting in line to be made-up. Stage hands are last-checking the scenery, while the prop crew reviews the placement of stage props and sets out hand props at entrances. On-stage electricians test overheads (Fresnels) and baby spots. Out front, house lights glow for the early birds who always come well ahead for choice seats. Other electricians are in place focusing and testing the front balcony spots with their colored gels.

You choose this time to give each member of your production staff your personal message of thanks and appreciation—a message handwritten by you on correspondence cards.

With the cards you hand your actors, include a typed memo, outlining the kind of pre-performance behavior that distinguishes the always-an-amateur from the professional (*professional* in the sense of being eager and proud to do the most skillful job possible).

Word your thanks any way you like, individualizing each note with the person's name and a suitable comment, however brief.

**Sample Appreciation to an Actor or a Crew Member**

Thank you, _____first name_____, for your loyalty and enthusiasm. The audience wants to enjoy our play. Give them a show to remember. Smile when you take your bow—you've earned that applause. Good luck!

Your signature

Let these 10 signs of the pro make up your memo to actors:

**The Real Pro:**

1. Gets into costume and make-up quickly and quietly.
2. Plays down "nerves" and tries to relax in spite of normal before-curtain jitters.
3. Doesn't nibble peanuts or down candy bars for energy or something to do. Such tidbits tend to back up and "Oops!" when they meet fluttery mid-region butterflies.
4. Stays backstage in the dressing room or in the wings. (The drinking fountain in the front hall and the lobby are out-of-bounds.)
5. *Never,* peeks through the curtain at the audience to see if Mom's there.
6. Takes a deep breath before stepping onstage "in character" and then stays "in character."
7. Never laughs at his own funny lines.
8. Knows how "to gravitate" toward the prompter in the wings if he forgets his own lines.
9. "Ad-libs" to cover a fellow actor in difficulty with his lines.
10. Improvises (stage business and/or lines) in any emergency, like a missed cue, a late entrance, or an off-time sound effect.

Your personal messages with your signature and perhaps also the typed memo for actors may find their way into scrapbooks and souvenir caches, to be brought out years from now by the recipients to relive a treasured memory, or to show their children or even their children's children.

*25 Minutes to C.T.:* You "gravitate" toward the lobby. The business manager is on the job, observing the front-of-the-house staff at work as the audience begins to arrive. The ticket-sales winner officiates well as the ticket taker. All programs are now in the hands of the ushers at their posts. The service club cake sale is attracting some of the arrivals to preview cakes and cookies and candy for purchase during the intermission or after the show.

The security officer stands impressively in view. The custodian is backstage now, to help if needed. Sales are slow at the box office, but they may pick up with late arrivals as curtain time nears. You definitely are not needed here. You glance into the auditorium. A musician is arranging sheet music at the piano. The rest of the musicians, now in the music room with the music director, are due to take their places with their instruments in 10 minutes. Things are moving along nicely.

*15 Minutes to C.T.:* Get backstage again to stay there. These last minutes are the most crucial of the pre-curtain period. The players are in the wings; the crews, in position. An electric tension charges the air, voices vibrate, eyes shine—that theatre magic is beginning to take over, providing a plus quality that sparks a splendid performance.

Should the wave of excitement crest too soon for any player and he or she burst into the jitters, be thankful. Stage fright is the best thing that can happen to an actor. Tell the actor so. Tell him that the jitters he feels set the actor apart from ordinary mortals. They keep the actor up, on his toes, making him exert extra effort— exactly what is needed to bring off a good performance. Confess that you're keyed up yourself, that jitters are a healthy sign in both of you.

*10 Minutes to C.T.:* The prompter with book is positioned in the wings. Actors take their places on set and offstage, ready for entrances. The special effects supervisor high signs you that all is okay with the phosphorescent head bit. You check. The nine-year-old substitute block and tackle is neatly tucked into the small area behind the set window. Happy beyond words to be a part of the show, she raises, then lowers the head, demonstrating how simple the job will be for her. You smile and promise to be on hand to cue her at the right moment. Now you can hear the musicians tuning up. All is well in the front of the house too.

*5 Minutes to C.T.:* The music begins. A hush falls backstage. Hardly a word is spoken. The music ends. Applause. Houselights dim. The magic moment has arrived.

### Curtain Time

The curtain opens. From now on, you remain backstage, but let the "playmakers," the actors and the stage crews run the show. You're satisfied that they should. As a professional yourself, a teacher, you know the special benefits every school playmaker derives from putting on a play—respect for his own skills, a greater understanding of his own value to himself as well as to others, and recognition from his parents, teachers and schoolmates. Isn't this what teaching is all about?

### Last Curtain Call

The curtain closes! The applause is spontaneous and enthusiastic. Curtain calls go smoothly, coming off just as you rehearsed them, right up to the last one with the entire production staff, including you, taking bows. Be prepared at this point, however, for something you haven't rehearsed. There's likely to be a surprise ending coming up.

It may take the form of a thank-you speech from the play's leading actor. It may be an orchid or a fine leather wallet, or maybe a nifty transistor radio—at any rate, some token (verbal or material) of appreciation for your efforts.

So be prepared. Try not to look too done-in. Your staff loves you. They want to share their triumph with you whether any present accompanies their thanks or not. Be gracious. Thank them for the loving thought. Then add to their brief moment of glory by commenting briefly yourself, if you think it suitable and if the audience seems to expect it, on the talented cast and the indefatigable crews you've had the joy of working with, and conclude by mentioning your personal satisfaction with the success of the play.

And now the curtain closes for the final time to more smiles, bows and applause, and the show is over.

## BAKER'S DOZEN STEPS FOR CLEANUP

Immediately (or the very next day) follow this baker's dozen steps for the cleanup:

1. Strike the set and store permanent set pieces.
2. Collect borrowed hand and stage props (furniture, clocks, rugs, etc.) for return to lenders within the week.—You may need to borrow again and promptness in returning items

establishes good will. Thank-you notes to lenders are also in order.

3. Store school-owned props.

4. Collect all borrowed and rented costumes and accessories for prompt return.

5. Store school-owned costumes.

6. Collect lighting, sound and special effects, and store.

7. Collect scripts and cue sheets for filing with the director's books and the prompter's book.

8. Clear the make-up table and tidy the make-up box.

9. Take down all posters around school advertising the play.

10. Leave the stage broom-clean.

11. Pick up discarded programs in the front of the house and the lobby.

12. Collect any articles forgotten by the audience and store them in the school's Lost and Found room.

13. Do anything else your particular situation demands. You are still the mastermind.

## AFTER-THE-PLAY WORK-PARTY

If some of the clean-up has to be postponed until the next day, turn the occasion into a kind of after-the-play work-party to help the stage crews who are obligated to report. Invite all the rest of the production staff, including the cast. The cast turnout will be good, for after a play is over the actors suffer very often a depressing let-down. flatter-than-flat feeling, as they return abruptly to the ordinariness of routine living. They'll welcome a return to the "scene of the crime." Serve light refreshments, stuff kids are supposed to like, but include juice, fresh fruit, carrot and celery sticks for those strong-minded enough to turn down soda, potato chips and brownies.

And now, it really is all over except for:

1. Settling financial matters when the business manager's report is turned over to you, and

2. Evaluating the production—its good and bad points—with an eye to being able to put on an even better play next time.

Whether the financial report shows a profit and whether or not your evaluation reveals more faults than virtues to the production, this you know—the production has fulfilled the purpose of any school play that is thoughtfully produced. It has offered every pupil who helped produce it first-hand experience with "theatre," an opportunity to be involved in a creative group activity and an ever-after increased appreciation of drama, which from its beginning 3000 years ago has been the mother of all performing arts and a continuing civilizing influence on the human spirit.

### Let's Review:

1. Before the performance be available backstage to help handle emergencies.
2. During the performance remain backstage but let your staff run the show.
3. After the performance be thorough in carrying out the clean-up.

A few lines back we mentioned "financial matters." Don't let the words scare you. They just meant that if tickets sold well, bringing in a big house, you may have turned a neat profit. You know, *profit*—What's left after you deduct production expenses from box-office take. Hallelujah!

Chapter 12 fills you in fully on all you need to know about financing any school play.

CHAPTER **12**

# How to Produce Your Play on a Shoestring—For Nothing or Next to Nothing

Financing your school play is as easy as one, two, three:

1. Keep accurate financial records.
2. Pay debts promptly.
3. Don't worry.

Money is the least of your problems. Treat money prudently, especially other people's, but spend what you must for what your play needs.

Now let's see what your minor expenditures in putting on a school play are, and then work out easy ways to meet these expenses.

With most lower school plays staged for such events as assembly programs or parent-teacher meetings, there is no, or at most a minimal, outlay of cash. Needs not readily met by school services, equipment and supplies are usually met by volunteer contributions of time, materials, and skills from parents and friends of the players. With productions involving older pupils—juniors (9-12) or young adults (12 and up)—performing for a paying audience, and sometimes for a nonpaying audience, certain basic expenditures on specific items are to be expected.

## TEN BASIC PRODUCTION EXPENSES

1. Royalty—it isn't professional to fudge on this fee; so pay it.
2. Scripts—this is another "must" if you're dealing with a play publisher.
3. Tickets ⎫
4. Programs ⎬ if commercially printed.
5. Publicity—most is free, but you may have to pay for art supplies.
6. Electrical supplies—gelatins, rentals of lighting equipment.
7. Scenery, properties, costumes—materials and rentals.
8. Make-up—cold cream, rouge, pencils, tissues, etc.
9. Overtime fees for custodian and for security officer.
10. Miscellaneous—last minute needs that always pop up; for example, you might have had to buy crepe paper for that hula skirt or bakery tarts for the Queen of Hearts in Chapter 11. Discretionary supplying of refreshments for the after-the-play work-party falls into this category too.

| NO-COSTS PRODUCTION | MINIMAL-COSTS PRODUCTION |
|---|---|
| And here's how to do it for— | |
| *NOTHING* | *Item* | *NEXT TO NOTHING* |

| NO-COSTS PRODUCTION | | MINIMAL-COSTS PRODUCTION |
|---|---|---|
| And here's how to do it for— | | |
| *NOTHING* | *Item* | *NEXT TO NOTHING* |
| (Well, on a shoestring) | | (—two shoestrings) |
| | *Royalty* | |
| Choose a royalty-free play; or use an original, unpublished play, where scripts can be typed by the school clerical staff. | | Choose a low-royalty play. |
| | *Playscripts* | |
| When you must buy scripts from a play publisher, run a food sale (for example, sell cake, bread or jelly contributed by parents, friends, players) to cover costs. Remember; you have a moral and legal obligation to the playwright. | | Order from the play publisher only as many copies as there are speaking parts (12 maximum); then run a food sale to cover the fee, if no sponsor (student government, service club, class, etc.) will advance the money, until you can pay the charges out of the box office take. |

| *NOTHING* | *Item* | *NEXT TO NOTHING* |
|---|---|---|
| | *Tickets* | |
| | *Programs* | |
| Cut corners here— no tickets no programs | | If these are professionally printed, costs can be paid out of the box office returns; otherwise, use school clerical services and duplicating equipment. |
| | *Publicity* | |
| | Use school talent and supplies. Newspaper and local radio publicity is free. | |
| | *Electrical Supplies and Equipment* | |
| Use what school equipment (lighting and sound) is available. | | Beg and borrow what you can; pay for rental and purchase of the rest out of the box office take. |
| | *Scenery, Props, Costumes and Make-up* | |
| Enlist outside help (parents, friends, local merchants) in supplying what the school drama wardrobe and storage closets cannot. Skip scenery (if necessary) and use only costumes and hand props. | | Borrow, rent, make or buy what is needed, and pay costs out of the box office take. |
| | *Custodian and Security Officer* | |
| Stage your play during the school day and eliminate these fees plus charges for the extra electric and heating costs that come out of the school budget. | | Not your responsibility, but that of your board of education. |
| | *Miscellaneous* | |
| Check with your principal. There's usually a school petty-cash box for needy cases. | | Pay from box office receipts. (Work-party refreshments could by your treat.) |

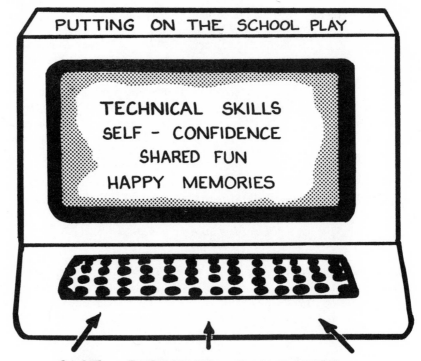

PUTTING ON THE SCHOOL PLAY

**INPUT AND OUTPUT**

**Putting on the School Play**

It takes a basic input—

| | | |
|---|---|---|
| cast | director | stage crew |
| costumes | playscript | lighting |
| dreams | stage | scenery |
| props | audience | sound effects |
| front-of-house staff | | teamwork |
| | | hard work |

To yield a generous output—

| | | |
|---|---|---|
| poise | new relationships | technical skills |
| grace of movement | drama appreciation | self-confidence |
| happy memories | entertainment | self-respect |
| discipline | understanding of | shared fun |
| social experience |   people | |

## That Does It!

Plunge into your production with the unfailing faith of the true artist, and somehow you'll find ways and means to finance it.

We've listed minor expenses. Major expenditures, of course, will be of your time, your energy and your talent, and the time, energy and talent of your production staff. These items, however, cannot be measured in terms of dollars and cents—as a professional teacher like you knows better than anyone else! The return on the major investment of these intangible assets, without doubt, more than balances any material costs.

Fortunately the director of a school play doesn't have to show a box office profit to stay in business, for the business of the school-play director is first, last and always children—their health, growth and happiness.

# INDEX